HIGHLIGHTS OF THE
WORLD SERIES

Yankee Stadium, New York

HIGHLIGHTS
OF THE
WORLD
SERIES

By JOHN DURANT

HASTINGS HOUSE PUBLISHERS • NEW YORK

To John McClain,
old friend and fellow-fan

Third edition, revised and enlarged, 1973
Second edition, revised and enlarged, 1971

Copyright © 1973, 1971, 1963 by John Durant

Library of Congress Cataloging in Publication Data

Durant, John, date   Highlights of the world series.

1.   World series (Baseball)   I. Title.
GV863.A1D87   1973   796.357'782   73-1619
ISBN 0-8038-3028-9

Published simultaneously in Canada by
Saunders of Toronto, Ltd., Don Mills, Ontario
Printed in the United States of America

Contents

Foreword

THE WORLD SERIES is America's greatest sports spectacle. It is seen or listened to by some fifty million persons, most of whom ordinarily take only a mild interest in baseball. It is the one sports event that grips the entire nation and holds it in thrall for a week.

It lures United States Presidents to the ball park, it crowds international events off the front pages of newspapers, it makes brothers of utter strangers standing three-deep at bars and it comes close to causing a nation-wide work stoppage in business and financial houses every October. It is reported by some 400 broadcasters and writers who annually turn out millions of words which describe in detail every move and gesture made on the ball field, as well as every sob and guffaw resounding in the clubhouse after the final game.

There is nothing in the world of sports quite like this stirring drama, which is rightly called the World Series, for it does in fact settle the championship of the world. Not many sports are represented by an undisputed champion, whether it be an individual or a team, but there is no doubt about the status of the winner of the World Series. It is the best baseball team in the world. It has gone through a hard six-month-long season to win the pennant in its league and then in its final test it has defeated the champions of the rival league. The proud title "World Champions" is well deserved and it is the hoped-for achievement of every baseball player in the major leagues.

The World Series has produced high moments of drama and of comedy. There have been sensational plays made in the Series — game-saving catches, grand-slam homers, an unassisted triple play, a no-hit, no-run perfect game, and breath-taking exhibitions of base stealing. There have been Series heroes and goats. Considering the caliber of the players, the Series has produced some very bad baseball. Almost every boner, blunder, and miscue known to the game has been committed in Series play. Perhaps this is one of the reasons for the widespread appeal of the Series. The players are, after all, human and under terrific pressure because they realize that their every action is being seen by millions on television as well as by thousands of fans in the stands. So it is understandable that what is known as the "Series jitters" may cause a player to throw to the wrong base, or not throw at all, or even run to an occupied base. Such things have happened and they will happen again.

Even the most experienced veterans are not immune to the shakes in the Series. "No matter how many times you go through it, it's always the same," said ex-Yankee catcher Bill Dickey, who played in eleven Series. "The strain sets in just before the first game, and it lasts all the way through. My stomach gets upset. My lips break out in fever blisters. I lie awake nights thinking about what's going to happen. Maybe I don't look nervous during a Series, but I sure do feel it."

Dickey spoke for most players when he said, "The pressure stays on until the final putout. You don't want the agony prolonged for even one more day. That's the way you feel in the World Series. The All-Star Game is nothing like it. You want to win it, and you want to do good . . . but it isn't the World Series. There's nothing like the World Series."

You're right, Bill, and there are fifty million people who agree with you. Let us hope that I have caught some of the drama and excitement of the Series on the pages that follow.

Introduction

THE BEGINNING OF THE WORLD SERIES

THE FIRST post-season set of games between championship baseball teams of two rival major leagues was staged in 1882, when the Cincinnati Reds met the Chicago White Stockings for what was announced as "the Baseball Championship of the World." The Reds were the pennant winners of the American Association and the White Stockings, forerunners of the present-day Chicago Cubs, were the champions of the National League.

This was the first World Series, although the term was not known at that time, and it came to an abrupt end after two games had been played. Nothing was settled. Each team won one game.

The leagues ignored each other in 1883 but resumed the playoffs the following year and continued to hold them annually until 1890. The American Association was disbanded at the end of the following season and the National League became the only major circuit in existence.

The National League-American Association Series of the nineteenth century were loosely organized, often inconclusive, and the rules governing them were changed from year to year. Some years, for example, the rival clubs played a best-of-five Series; in other years it was best-of-seven and sometimes they went on barnstorming trips and played ten or more games in several cities.

In 1887, a banner year for barnstorming, Detroit and St. Louis, respective champions of the National League and the American Association, played fifteen games in ten cities, including Boston, Brooklyn, Chicago, and Pittsburgh. On October 21 the clubs played a doubleheader, each game in a different city — Baltimore in the morning and Washington in the afternoon. Such were the so-called World Series of yesteryear.

From 1891 to 1903 there were, perhaps mercifully, no more interleague playoffs. Following are the results of the National League-American Association Series:

1882 — Chicago (N.L.) won 1 game; Cincinnati (A.A.) won 1 game.

1883 — No Series.

1884 — Providence (N.L.) won 3 games; New York Metropolitans (A.A.) won none.

1885 — Chicago (N.L.) won 3 games; St. Louis (A.A.) won 3 games; 1 tie, no playoff.

1886 — St. Louis (A.A.) won 4 games; Chicago (N.L.) won 2 games.

1887 — Detroit (N.L.) won 10 games; St. Louis (A.A.) won 5 games.

1888 — New York Giants (N.L.) won 6 games; St. Louis (A.A.) won 4 games.

1889 — New York Giants (N.L.) won 6 games; Brooklyn (A.A.) won 3 games.

1890 — Brooklyn (N.L.) won 3 games; Louisville (A.A.) won 3 games; 1 tie, no playoff.

CHAPTER 1

THE FIRST REAL WORLD SERIES
(1905)

IT WAS 1905, a year to remember. It was the year that President Teddy Roosevelt put a stop to the Russo-Japanese War by arranging a peace conference in this country between the two warring nations. Down in Panama that year United States engineers were digging a canal across the isthmus. Elihu Root, one of our greatest statesmen, became Secretary of State; world heavyweight champion Jim Jeffries, who had whipped everybody in sight, announced, "I'll never fight again," and hung up his gloves. (In a comeback attempt five years later he was knocked flat by Jack Johnson.) The darling of the stage that year was Blanche Bates, a sparkling blonde who starred in *The Girl of the Golden West*. The movies produced its first star in "Broncho Billy" Anderson, a dashing cowboy in the nickelodeons, who was born Max Aronson in Brooklyn.

It was a golden year all the way, especially in the baseball world. It was the year the first World Series was played — the first *real* World Series, at any rate.

True, there had been a sort of Series two years before in 1903 when the National and American League champions (Pittsburgh and Boston) met in a post-season playoff which Boston won by five games to three. It was a pick-up Series, though, an informal challenge match without the sanction of organized baseball and was, therefore, un-official. Furthermore, it was a one-shot affair which began and ended that year. No Series were played on either side of it, in 1902 or 1904.

The reason was that the long-established National League (founded in 1876) was unwilling to recognize the recently formed (in 1901) American League as an equal. For two years there had been a bitter and exhausting baseball war which included player raids by both leagues, law suits and name-calling in the press. Even when truce was declared in 1903 and the American League had come of age, there were still a number of National Leaguers who loathed the "upstarts," as they called the newcomers, and vowed that they would never have anything to do with them.

One of the most outspoken of these National League diehards was John J. McGraw, the fiery manager of the New York Giants, who was only 31 years old in 1904 when his team won the pennant. Boston had won the American League race again and, as it did the year before, challenged the National League winner to settle things in a post-season playoff.

McGraw spat in Boston's face with a reply so strong that the newspapers did not dare print it, not even the racy *Police Gazette*. He was seconded in similar terms by John T. Brush, his boss, owner of the Giants.

Both had their reasons for detesting the upstarts. McGraw, a National Leaguer for many years with the Baltimore Orioles, became the club's playing manager when it switched to the American League in 1901. Suspicious and quarrelsome, McGraw found himself at odds with Byron Bancroft (Ban) Johnson, president and founder of the new league. In June, 1902, he jumped the Orioles and came to New York, once more a National Leaguer and a dedicated foe of the rival circuit and everyone in it.

Brush loathed the newcomers because they had set up shop right in his own city with a new club and a new ball park and he was feeling it at the box office. What's more, the team was loaded with ex-National Leaguers who had crossed over. The New York Americans were originally known as the Highlanders because their park was on one of the highest points in Manhattan. That name was too long for headline writers, so one day a New York reporter became angry and called them the Yankees. The name stuck.

The McGraw-Brush turndown gave the American Leaguers plenty of ammunition to fire at their rivals. "Afraid of us, aren't you?" they taunted. "We licked you last year and we can lick you any time."

Finally a compromise was effected when some of the more far-sighted members of the old league realized that the American League was here to stay. By 1905 a set of rules was drawn up and approved by the three-man National Commission, then the governing body of major-league baseball. The most important rule stated that the playing of the Series would be compulsory, that the champions of the two leagues would *have* to meet after the regular season. Thus it came about that the first real World Series was born, under rules that still regulate the annual spectacle after more than half a century of continuous play without interruption.

John J. McGraw, as short of temper as he was of body (he stood only 5 feet 7 inches), and his swaggering Giants were ready that fall for the Philadelphia Athletics, winners of the American League flag. The players were in good shape and eager to have a go at those upstarts down in Philadelphia.

Brush had special uniforms made for his boys. Nobby outfits they were, too — jet-black suits with the large white lettering "N.Y." across the chest, white stockings, and white box caps with black visors. New York went crazy over the Giants. They were paraded, banquets were given for them, they were received at City Hall. Prominent figures of the theatrical and sporting world got together and threw a testimonial banquet for them. Those were McGraw's pals, the Broadway bunch — high steppers like Tod Sloan, the famous jockey; Gentleman Jim Corbett, the ex-heavyweight champion; George M. Cohan, song writer and actor; Jack Doyle, the bookmaker. (McGraw was a devoted horse player all his life.)

The team reflected McGraw's image. It was fast and tough and would do anything to win. That was McGraw. He was of the old blood-and-guts school of baseball, made famous by the Baltimore Orioles. That is where he had learned his trade in the nineties, where he and his teammates had first developed inside baseball — the squeeze play, the bunt, the double steal and the hit-and-run play, all mixed in with every kind of trickery and dodge, the bullying of opponents, and umpire-baiting. The idea was to win at all costs.

Years later McGraw was to say that his 1905 team was the best he ever saw or heard of. One of his moundsmen was Iron Man Joe McGinnity, a rubber-armed, underhand artist with a tantalizing up-curve. He earned his nickname by pitching double-headers, his specialty. In one month in 1903 he pitched and won three double-headers for the Giants. He was more than a marathon hurler, though. He won thirty-five games and lost only eight in 1904, his best year. His receiver was Roger Bresnahan, who was smart and fleet-footed, fast enough to bat leadoff. He was, incidentally, the first backstop to use shin guards. Shortstop Bill Dahlen and Art Devlin, who played third, were tough competitors. The outfield was fast and reliable. But the greatest of them all, the dazzling gem in the Giant crown, was the big handsome collegian, Christy Mathewson. He was perhaps the finest pitcher the National League has ever known.

Matty had been an outstanding athlete at Bucknell, where he'd played baseball and football. A right-hander, he was a brilliant student of baseball, shrewd and cool under fire. He had a good fast ball and his control was uncanny. He had stuff that no other pitcher ever had. The big tousled-haired pitching idol stood over 6 feet and weighed close to 200 pounds. He threw overhand and had a beautiful curve that broke around the knees. He also had a super-duper known as the fadeaway. It required a reverse twist of the wrist and the ball seemed to twist, too, as it spun toward the plate. Many a batsman who went down swinging at it would return to his dugout with head shaking in utter disbelief, looking like the storied farmer who has just seen his first giraffe and knows it can't be real. The pitch was the opposite of the screwball that Carl Hubbell, a southpaw, threw years later with much the same effect. Year after year Matty won twenty or more games and for three consecutive seasons (1903–1905) he won thirty or more. Everybody knew that McGraw would start him against the A's in the forthcoming Series. The big fellow had just finished the 1905 campaign with a 31–9 won-lost record and he was ready.

If two men were ever unlike, they were John J. McGraw and Connie Mack, the manager of the Philadelphia Athletics. Born Cornelius Alexander McGillicuddy, the former catcher had come up through the baseball ranks in the rough and tough days when the chest protector was unknown and the catcher was the only man who wore a glove — an ordinary kid glove, at that, but with the fingers cut off. The game in his day was not for sissies. It had a full quota of tough, hard-eyed pros and it was rated just a notch above the bare-knuckle prize ring, an outlaw sport, on the social ladder.

14

JOSEPH JEROME McGINNITY
"IRONMAN"
DISTINGUISHED AS THE PITCHER WHO HURLED
TWO GAMES ON ONE DAY THE MOST TIMES. DID
THIS ON FIVE OCCASIONS. WON BOTH GAMES
THREE TIMES. PLAYED WITH BALTIMORE,
BROOKLYN AND NEW YORK TEAMS IN N.L.
AND BALTIMORE IN A.L. GAINED MORE THAN
200 VICTORIES DURING CAREER. RECORDED
20 OR MORE VICTORIES SEVEN TIMES. IN TWO
SUCCESSIVE SEASONS WON AT LEAST 30 GAMES.

Iron Man Joe McGinnity, the tireless Giant hurler, is enshrined in the Baseball Hall of Fame at Cooperstown, New York. Above is his plaque.

It did not harden Connie Mack, though. He was gentle, soft-spoken and patient. He never swore, never smoked, and he drank very sparingly. He managed the A's for fifty years and was never once thrown out of a game. Tall and frail, he always wore street clothes on the field. He looked the same in 1905 at the age of 42 as he did forty-five years later when he finally quit the bench.

Connie was the first manager to seek out college men for his clubs. He put together some fine teams and some weak ones, but in general they reflected his character in that they were harmonious and likable. That was the 1905 team, a strong one with many collegians. There were some colorful boys on it, however, who never got through grade school.

One was Rube Waddell, the best left-hander in baseball when he wasn't chasing fire engines, fishing, standing behind a bar, or smashing straw hats. Those were his favorite pastimes. Rube was the kid who never grew up. Every year he looked forward eagerly to September 1, the day that summer straw hats were traditionally discarded and forgetful wearers ran the risk of having them broken by pranksters. Rube loved to go around looking for straw hats on that day. On September 1, 1905, on a station platform, he spotted one on the head of Andy Coakley, a fellow-pitcher on the A's. Rube went after Andy's hat. Andy ran, Rube chased him down the platform, tripped over some luggage and fell heavily on his left arm. It stiffened up that night. He tried a couple of starts after that, but he had nothing and Connie knew that he was out of the Series.

Almost as wild as the Rube was his catcher and roommate, Ossee Schreckengost, who caught one-handed and looked like a Dutch burlesque comic. In the outfield Connie's big gun was Socks Seybold, a tremendous home-run hitter for those days. His sixteen homers in 1902 was a league record until Babe Ruth shattered it with twenty-nine in 1919. Oddly, two players named Cross, Lave and Monte, who were unrelated, played next to each other on the left side of the infield.

One of Connie's aces was Charles Albert Bender, who was called Albert by the ever-polite manager but was called Chief by the rest of the world (he was part Chippewa). The Chief learned to pitch at the Carlisle Indian School in Pennsylvania. A big right-hander about the same size as Matty, he was a great money pitcher and an excellent

16

hitter. He was reserved and gentlemanly. Nothing ever seemed to bother the Chief. When fans joshed him with Indian war whoops, he would josh them right back by turning to the stands and yelling, "Foreigners! Foreigners!"

Rumors began to fly around about Rube Waddell just before the Series started. "Why wasn't he playing? Had the gamblers paid him to pull out of the Series?" the sports asked in pool rooms and saloons along Broadway. "Look, he's the best southpaw in the world and Mack pays him only $2,200 for a full year's work. No wonder he sold out."

There was no truth in the rumors. The Rube's teammates knew there wasn't, angry as they were with him because of his juvenile behavior. His arm wasn't the only thing that had been hurt. Their chances of beating the Giants had been hurt also.

A few days before the Series' opening day, October 9, a more suspicious thing than mere rumors took place. The players of both teams got together and most of them agreed to split their Series pay on a 50–50 basis regardless of which team won.* The system used was to pair off player for player, each pair to make its own agreement. Most pairs decided on the even split, instead of the division set by the new official Series rules. This was 75 per cent to the winners, 25 per cent to the losers. (The players' purse came from 60 per cent of the gross receipts from the first four games of the four-out-of-seven Series.)

There was nothing crooked about these man-to-man deals. The players were going all out to win, no matter what the gate was or the division of the spoils. They simply thought that the 75–25 split set by the rules was too wide** and they wanted to be sure of a decent purse, win or lose. After all, the average player's salary then was less than $3,000 and the greatest stars drew down only about $3,500. Just the same, such a deal would not be tolerated today.

Young Andy Coakley, two years out of Holy Cross, was paired with Christy Mathewson at the meeting. "What do you say, Matty? How will we split it?" he asked the great one.

"Well," reflected the cool, blue-eyed Matty, "let's wait a bit. Let's wait until after the first game and see how things are."

* A common practice today among professional golfers wherein two finalists of a tournament privately agree to divide evenly the total amount of the purse for first and second places.
** The rule-makers agreed with the players on this in 1907 and made the split 60–40, which it is today.

He knew how things would be, all right. He knew that he was right, that no one on earth was going to beat him, so why give away a chunk of his purse? As it turned out, Matty was better than unbeatable in that Series. He was untouchable. He put together three pitching masterpieces such as had never been seen before and were never to be seen again.

Here is what the superb one did in a period of six days: he blanked the A's three times for a total of twenty-seven scoreless innings, yielding only fourteen hits, walking only one man, and striking out eighteen. And the A's, mind you, were noted as a hitting team.

"It was just unbelievable," said Andy Coakley years later, as he recalled the feat with reverence. "When it was over, Matty and I split 75–25 just like the rule book ordered. Well, I couldn't pitch with him and I couldn't make a deal with him but I did all right, anyway, because the whole Athletic team divided their money equally among themselves in the end."

Gettysburg Eddie Plank, a collegian, was Matty's victim in the opening game which was played in a bandbox of a ball park in Philadelphia's brewery section before about 18,000 fans, nearly half of whom were standees.

Gettysburg Eddie turned in a good game, allowing three runs, but he was no match for Matty who gave up only four hits. In true McGraw style, the Giants exhibited their speed and daring. They stole four bases on Ossee Schreckengost, who may have been thinking about his missing roommate, the Rube.

A large gong had been installed near the Broad Street Station in the heart of Philadelphia for the benefit of the fans. It was to be rung once for Philadelphia two-base hits, twice for triples, and three times for homers made by the A's. The bell-ringer, as it turned out, had one of the softest jobs in the land that week. In the whole Series he rang it only five times — for five doubles. There were no Philadelphia triples or homers.

Back to the depot went the happy New York fans, in hacks and trolleys. The next day they reassembled at the Polo Grounds to watch the Iron Man hurl against Chief Bender, the 22-year-old Chippewa. A crowd of 24,992 was on hand for this one.

The Chief had his day, and Philadelphia's only day, on that Tuesday, October 10. The big town and the wildly screaming crowd

John J. McGraw, fiery manager of the Giants for more than thirty years
(1901–1932) brought New York its first World Championship in 1905.
Right, Christy Mathewson, an all-time great, was perhaps the finest pitcher
the National League has produced.

did not faze the Indian. He duplicated Matty's feat of the previous
day, allowing only four hits and winning, 3–0. Now it was one and
one and the A's had hope.

They did not expect to face Matty again until the fourth game,
but it rained all day Wednesday and the next day in Philadelphia,
there was Matty on the hill. He zeroed the A's again, 9 to 0, and struck
out eight. "Matty was off form today," said one Giant fan jokingly.

"Yeah, he walked a man." That was the only time he did in the entire Series.

The National Commission decreed that the next two games would be played in New York, thus assuring a Saturday date for the larger Polo Grounds. Even in those days baseball magnates were well aware of the box office.

It was a tight pitching duel all the way between Gettysburg Eddie and the Iron Man, but the A's managed to blow the game in the fourth when a grounder was muffed by shortstop Monte Cross, and two plays later another grounder went through the bowed legs of Lave Cross. The two miscues by the two Crosses gave the Giants their only run and the ball game. The A's were crushed and their tempers were not improved any by the fact that while the worst was happening in the fourth, the carefree Rube was sitting at one end of the bench reading a magazine. Poor Eddie Plank had allowed only four hits but he was the 1–0 loser.

Another big crowd jammed the Polo Grounds the next day to see Matty wrap it up. He was pitching with only one day's rest, but it mattered not. He mowed them down as usual, one after another. His opponent, Chief Bender, allowed one hit less than Matty (five to six) and struck out the same number, but he suffered a brief loss of control and walked two men in the fifth. A sacrifice moved them up and a deep fly brought in a run. Another Giant run came in the ninth. The final score was 2 to 0. Matty had run his collection of World Series goose eggs to twenty-seven. His final masterpiece was finished in 1 hour and 35 minutes.

They played a different brand of baseball in those days, before the ball was souped up. The accent was on finesse and precision, on pitching artistry, base running, and place hitting, rather than toe-hold slugging. It was tight, clever baseball as a rule, quite unlike today's power-hitting marathons that often run more than three hours. In the 1905 World Series each game was finished in less than two hours and not a home run was hit.

This is not to say that every game in the old days was fast and flawless. Indeed, teams often went to pieces and booted the ball all over the park. In the third Series game, for example, the A's made five errors (three by second baseman Dan Murphy). In the main, however, errors were few, scores were low, and the pace was fast.

After the final game McGraw left the clubhouse with a phalanx of bodyguards and was escorted to the Broadway tenderloin district, his favorite beat. He took bows, made speeches, and gloated, "The American Leaguers said we were afraid to play them. Well, what do they say now? I say we're champions of the only real big league. The Series proves it."

Ecstatic Broadway crowds followed him around chanting the popular song of the day, *Tammany*, the final line of which went:

Tammany, Tammany — swamp 'em, swamp 'em, get that wampum — Tammany!

The Giants swamped 'em, all right, but did they get the wampum? Their official shares came to $1,142, those of the A's to a paltry $370. However, Connie Mack persuaded his boss, Ben Shibe, owner of the Athletics, to toss the club's share of the receipts into the players' pot. This brought the individual Athletic shares up to $823.22.

In addition, there were those side arrangements made between the players of the two clubs. When the Giants settled up, their shares went down and the A's went up. In the end the boys from Philadelphia made more money than the World Champions.

When McGraw heard about this he was livid — not because of the secret deal and the questionable ethics, but because his players had not shown complete faith in themselves and in Matty.

This early Polo Grounds scene shows Roger Bresnahan, catcher for the Giants, with Joe Tinker, Chicago Cubs infielder, at bat.

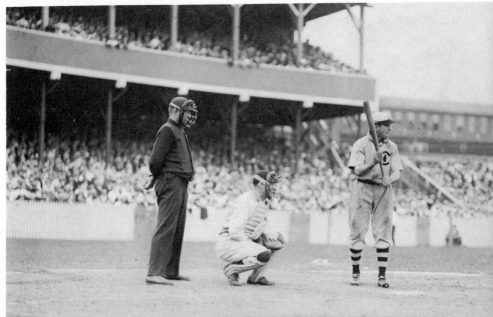

CHAPTER 2

COBB AND WAGNER MEET

(1906–1913)

SOMETHING ELSE happened in 1905 besides the first real World Series, the end of the Russo-Japanese War, and plans for the digging of the Panama Canal. Scarcely anyone was aware of it at the time, though, and there was no reason why anyone should have been. It was a quiet, unspectacular event but it had great significance in baseball history.

It was the year that a steel-muscled 18-year-old rookie made his big-league debut as an outfielder with the Detroit Tigers. He came from Georgia, this light-haired six-footer, and his name was Tyrus Raymond Cobb. He played only forty-one games in 1905. He hit a homer, stole two bases, and batted an undistinguished .240.

That was the beginning of the most incredible career in the annals of the game. For the next twenty-three years Ty Cobb played every season and never again batted under .300. He finished in 1928 at 41 with a .323 average for that season and a lifetime mark of .367, the highest ever compiled by any player. Three seasons he batted better than .400 and year after year he led the league in just about everything — batting averages, stolen bases, most hits made, most runs scored. For twenty-four years he played every game as if his life depended upon it. There has never been a ball player with his skills and his competitive drive.

Baseball's greatest player was human, however. He was not completely unstoppable, especially in World Series play. Ty played in three Series (1907, 1908, 1909) and stood out in only one, in 1908. In the other two he was ordinary, which is not surprising. For the Series have a way of lowering the great and bringing forth the unknown for a brief bow in the spotlight.

That happened in 1906, the year the Chicago Cubs ran away with the National League flag by winning a record 116 games and finishing twenty games ahead of the second-place Giants, who had met with a series of injuries. Oddly, the American League finish was also Chicago first, New York second, but there was only a three-game spread between them.

The Chicago White Sox had been lucky to win, said the experts. They had fair pitching, yes, but they were miserable at the plate. They were known as the "Hitless Wonders" and with good reason. The team's batting average was .228, which was next to last in the league, and their top hitter, "Bald Eagle" Isbell, the second baseman, was good for only .279. How could these weaklings ever hope to beat the runaway Cubs? It did not seem possible. To a man the dopesters picked the Cubs, with the sole exception of Hughie Fullerton, a baseball writer on the *Chicago Tribune*.

Fullerton sat down on the eve of the Series, took a look at the crystal ball, and saw the White Sox winning. Not only that, he wrote down a game-by-game forecast, calling the turn on every contest. His city editor at first refused to print it, but he changed his mind just in time and the prediction appeared in the newspaper before the first game.

To the astonishment of everybody, the games were won and lost in the order that Fullerton had called them. Six games were played and the Hitless Wonders won four and lost two.

What Fullerton did not forecast (and who can blame him?) was the role played by a substitute infielder named George Rohe who was in great part responsible for the White Sox victory. Less than ordinary, with a season batting average of .254, Rohe would not have played at all had not the regular shortstop, George Davis, been injured just before the first game. Rohe stepped in and went wild.

His triple in the first game was the deciding punch in a 2–1 victory. In the third game he socked another triple for all the runs the Sox needed to win, 3–0. In the fifth and sixth games he put the Cubs out of business with five hits that wrapped up the title for the Sox. He hit way over his head in the Series, batting .333. The following season his average was .213. That was his last year in the majors. Down to New Orleans and to minor-league obscurity went George Rohe, the first flash in the pan in Series history. There were to be more like him.

Hughie Fullerton had his big day, too, in the 1906 Series. For years thereafter he capitalized on his once-in-a-million bull's-eye and sold his pre-Series forecasts to newspapers throughout the country. He never hit it like that again. He was no better, no worse than the general run of baseball dopesters.

It was 1907 and along came Ty Cobb with the pennant-winning Detroit Tigers ready to battle the Cubs, again champions of the National League. That season Ty had won his first American League batting title with .350 and he also led the league in stolen bases (49) and most hits (212). The 20-year-old thunderbolt was the talk of the baseball world.

One of his teammates was a light-hearted infielder named Herman (Germany) Schaefer who, when he wasn't clowning (he once stole first base from second in a regular league game just for laughs), represented the players in their dealings with baseball's brass.

In a pre-Series meeting with the National Commission, Germany put an interesting question before the moguls about players sharing in the gate receipts of the first four Series games only — a rule, incidentally, that exists today. "Suppose," asked Germany, "one of those games is a tie. Do we get a share of that one in addition to the four games that go to a decision, or does the tie game count as one of the first four?"

The three commissioners put their heads together and after much pondering gave Germany their answer: "If a tie should occur, the players will share in the first five games." The story was given much space on the front pages of the Chicago newspapers on the morning of the first game.

That afternoon the game ended in a 3–3 tie. Needless to say, there was much eyebrow-lifting over that one. Understandably, a great many fans were convinced that the game had been rigged to end in a tie. The Commission was furious. An investigation followed. A review of the questionable game revealed that both teams had fought hard to

Ty Cobb, Detroit's super-star and the game's greatest hitter and base-stealer, played for twenty-four years and achieved a lifetime batting average of .367, the highest ever compiled.

win and that there had been several battles and much name-calling between the two clubs. Therefore, decided the Commission, the tie game was no more than coincidence.

It probably was, at that. It seems incredible that if the players were going to fix a game, they would do it so soon after the widely publicized decision of the Commission. Just the same, the commissioners ruled that in all future Series the players would share in the first four games only, no matter how they ended. They stood by their promise to Schaefer, however, and let the athletes cut in on the full five games.

That is all there was to the 1907 Series — five games, counting the tie. The Cubs won four games without a loss. Ty Cobb fared poorly, batting a mere .200.

In 1908 it was the Cubs and the Tigers again. Glorying in their third consecutive National League championship, the Cubs had an outstanding team, possibly the first great one of this century despite what John McGraw always said about his 1905 Giants.

Frank Chance, manager and first baseman, filled both jobs superbly and was affectionately called the "Peerless Leader." Johnny Evers, a flashy 125-pounder, was on second, and Joe Tinker, fast and versatile, played next to him at short. The fact that Tinker and Evers had a bitter feud going and did not speak a word to each other for many years, made no difference in the brand of play they turned in. The three infielders made a fine combination and became famous for making double plays.

Franklin P. Adams, a New York newspaper columnist and Giant fan, immortalized the trio with a jingle, the first four lines of which are:

These are the saddest of possible words
Tinkers to Evers to Chance.
Trio of Bear Cubs and fleeter than birds,
Tinkers to Evers to Chance.

The Cubs had a strong pitching staff, which was led by Mordecai (Three Finger) Brown, an ex-farm boy who had lost most of the index finger of his right hand in a corn-shredder. It was a lucky accident, as it turned out. Three Finger made good use of the stub in baseball. It enabled him to put an extra fillip on the ball and throw a fantastically wide curve. Brown was the only pitcher who had it over Christy Mathewson in man-to-man pitching duels. The two masters met each other twenty-four times in league games between 1904 and 1916, and Three Finger had the edge by two games, winning thirteen to Matty's eleven. Curiously, when the two rivals faced each other for the final time, on September 4, 1916, it was the last big-league game for both.

The Detroit club was managed by Hughie Jennings who had played on the old Baltimore Orioles with John McGraw. In the tradition of the Orioles, the Tigers were a tough, aggressive bunch. In center field next to Ty Cobb, who then played right field, was Wahoo Sam Crawford, a consistent .300 hitter. (In 1907 Wahoo Sam was runner-up to the terrible Ty for the league batting championship with .323.) The unusual nickname was given Sam because of his birthplace, Wahoo, Nebraska.

Ty Cobb had his day in the 1908 Series but it wasn't enough to beat the Cubs. The Tigers won only one game, the second one, and were the losers by four games to one. Ty got seven hits in nineteen tries for a batting average of .368 and stole two bases. He was blanked in the last two games, however. In all, it was a rather drab Series. It was cold and raw most of the time and the bad weather held down the crowd, especially in Detroit which was not much of a baseball town, anyway. The Tigers failed to score a run in the last two games, both of which were held in Detroit. A low attendance record was set in the fifth and final game when only 6,210 chilled fans showed up to watch the death blow. It was the poorest crowd in World Series history.

Fans were beginning to wonder about the American League. Maybe it was just a good minor league, after all, they said. Outside of that lucky win by the Hitless Wonders in 1906, the Americans had shown nothing, said the fans. The low ebb was still to come, however. There was one more year of humiliation in store for the American League and after that the tide turned.

The year the new league struck bottom was 1909. The Tigers took the flag again, making it three in a row, but the Cubs were no longer on top of the National League. The pennant was won by the Pittsburgh Pirates, a new wonder team whose key man was one of the all-time greats.

He was John Peter Wagner, who was called Hans or Honus and sometimes the Flying Dutchman. No matter what he was called, Wagner was perhaps the greatest all-round player in the game's history. He did everything but catch and he was one of the most feared right-handers who ever came to bat.

There was much more interest in the 1909 Series than there had been the year before. One reason was that baseball's two outstanding stars, Cobb and Wagner, were going to meet head on. Both were the batting champions of their respective leagues — Cobb with .377, Wag-

Hans Wagner (both photos) starred for Pittsburgh at shortstop, but he could play any position. The National League batting champion for eight years, Hans clashed with Ty Cobb in the 1909 Series.

ner with .339. Both were terrors on the base paths and were second to none as defensive players. Hans played shortstop.

Many years later when the first ballots were cast by the Baseball Writers' Association for membership in the Baseball Hall of Fame at Cooperstown, New York, only five players were elected. Ty Cobb and Hans Wagner were two of the five. Christy Mathewson, Walter Johnson, and Babe Ruth were the others. That was the core, the foundation, the beginning of a long list to come in the following years — the result of much deliberation and ballot-casting. But there was no question about the first five. No debate was possible. They were the greatest and that was that.

Hans Wagner and Ty Cobb were opposites in everything but playing ability. Cobb was a firebrand, continually fighting with his opponents, with umpires, and even with members of his own team. He was ruthless on the base paths and would not hesitate to cut a man down with his always-sharp spikes. Honus, on the other hand, was easy-going and likable and would never think of spiking a player in an attempted steal. He was one of the most inoffensive players ever to wear a major-league uniform.

Broad-shouldered, bow-legged, and with big ham-like hands, Honus was on the awkward side but he could move fast. He had enough speed to lead the National League in stolen bases for five years, and he was the league's batting champion for eight years. He had a horse-whip arm and covered a wide range around short. John McGraw often named him as the greatest player of all time. So did Edward Barrow, the architect of the Yankee dynasty, who, like McGraw, had seen them all — Cobb, Ruth, Speaker, Hornsby, Gehrig, Sisler, and other super stars.

The meeting of the two greats took place in Pittsburgh on October 8, 1909, when the rival clubs appeared for pre-game practice. A photographer asked the two batting champions to pose at home plate, with Hornus on one side as a right-hander and the left-hander Cobb on the other side. They shook hands — it was their first meeting — and then struck hitting postures.

Each looked at the other's grip on the bat and in amazement they realized that they were doing exactly the same thing. It was an unusual grip and each had developed it without being taught. They held the bats with their hands four or five inches apart and with the lower hand about a palm-width above the end of the bat handle. Only a very few players have ever used this grip and none was a batter of any importance except these two. Here were the two best hitters in baseball, completely unlike in character, physique, and temperament. Yet they had adopted this identical and distinctive grip.

The only time the two stars ever met in formal combat, Wagner outran Cobb, outhit him by .333 to .231, and the Pirates won the Series, four games to three. The outcome of the running duel was a big surprise, for Ty had led the American League that season with seventy-six stolen bases and Honus at the age of 35 was beyond his peak and had a touch of rheumatism. Still, he was fast and crafty.

The first time Cobb got on base he cupped his hands and yelled at Wagner, "Hey, Krauthead, I'm coming down on the next pitch." Hans nodded but said nothing. Sure enough, Ty took off with the pitch but when he got to second Hans had the ball and slapped it into Ty's mouth. Ty was out and had a swollen lip to boot.

Cobb was himself again the next day and he electrified the crowd by stealing home. He was one of the few to accomplish this in a World Series. The third game was a Wagnerian triumph. The bow-legged German-American got on base five times and attempted five steals. The Tigers got him out only once. He wound up the day with three steals and in the remaining try he made second safely but failed to get credit for a stolen base because Charley Schmidt, the Tiger catcher, dropped the ball and did not throw to second.

In the fifth game Honus practically stole a run. He was hit by a pitched ball and got on first. He stole second; he stole third and then continued on home when the harried Schmidt threw over the third baseman's head.

It was a running World Series, all right, with the aptly named Flying Dutchman leading the way. The Pirates stole eighteen bases in all, which was a record, and that was as much a factor in their victory as the pitching of Babe Adams, a rookie with a 12–3 won-lost record for the season.

It was more Adams' show than anyone else's, Cobb and Wagner included. The twenty-six-year-old freshman was rated fourth on the Pirate pitching staff, behind the club's big three: Howard Camnitz (25–6), Vic Willis (22–12), and Lefty Leifield (19–8). Adams pitched and won three full games, an unheard-of feat for a rookie. The fourth Pirate triumph, strangely enough, was credited to Nick Maddox, a 13–8 performer. None of the big three won a game. Adams' name became known across the nation.

Attendance shot way up in this Series. It was on the threshold of becoming a national event, rather than an intercity affair with interest largely confined to the two cities involved.

It was the last World Series for Cobb and Wagner. They never clashed again but they saw each other often and became friends. The Dutchman finished out his career in 1917 with a lifetime batting average of .329. For years the amiable old fellow was a Pirate coach. He died poor in 1955. Ty Cobb died a multi-millionaire in 1961, cantankerous, quick-tempered, and full of fight to the end.

The American League had struck bottom, but it was not long before things began to look up for the newcomers. It started in 1910 when Connie Mack produced the new league's first great team and won two consecutive Series.

Connie's young and spirited team faced the Cubs in 1910 and to the astonishment of most fans, including Hughie Fullerton who had picked the Cubs, not only did the A's win but they won with only two pitchers. They were Chief Bender, who was then at his zenith with a 23–5 season, and big Jack Coombs of Colby College in Maine who had just completed a sensational 31–9 campaign. These two did it all. They pitched every inning of every one of the five games played. The Chief won one and lost one while Jack Coombs turned in three victories to give the A's the World Championship, four games to one.

It was the A's again the following year (1911), but this time they faced their old rivals, the Giants. This Series was notable for two things. One was the longest rain ever to wash out a sports event of national interest. It started falling on October 18 after the third game and did not let up for five days. When it finally did, the Philadelphia ball park was a quagmire and an extra day was needed to dry it off, by a crew burning gasoline cans night and day. Play was resumed on October 24, six days later than scheduled.

The other event was the sudden rise to fame of the A's third baseman, Frank Baker. In 1911 he won the American League home-run crown with nine, a paltry figure by today's standards, but Baker was hitting a dead, tobacco-juice-stained ball. In the Series he got two homers on successive days in the second and third games, both of them off McGraw's pitching aces — Rube Marquard and Christy Mathewson. From then on he was known to everyone as Home Run Baker.

The homer off Matty was particularly galling to the big hurler. That morning the newspapers had carried a story signed by Matty (but undoubtedly written by his ghost writer) which criticized Marquard for allowing the homer the day before in the second game. "Rube should never have thrown Baker a fast ball," wrote Matty via his ghost. That afternoon only a few hours after the story appeared, up to the plate came Frank Baker and boom! Matty was it. The next morning Rube's ghost got to work in the newspapers and asked, "What happened, Matty? It couldn't be that you grew careless, or did you?"

The Matty-Marquard tiff did not improve the club's morale. McGraw's men won two games and lost four. Frank Baker was the high man of both clubs in batting with .375. The low man was the Giants' clean-up hitter, right fielder Jack Murray who had hit .291 for the season. In the Series Red played all six games, came to bat twenty-one times, and wound up with a batting average of .000.

After the Series Rube Marquard and his wife, a popular night club songstress named Blossom Seely, teamed up in a vaudeville act in New York. The Rube had no stage experience but because he was a Giant hero his wife thought that their act would draw well. On the stage the two exchanged banter and the Rube joined her in a ballad or two. The act did not last long, not after one critic wrote of it: "Marquard can sing as well as Caruso can pitch."

Rube stuck to his trade and had a phenomenal season in 1912. Starting on opening day, the big gangling left-hander (he stood 6 feet, 3 inches and weighed 180 pounds) won nineteen consecutive games and was not beaten until July 7. He faded toward the end of the season, however, losing eleven of his last eighteen games for a record of 26–11. Rube was a big factor in bringing the flag to the Giants that year. The club finished ten games in front of the second-place Pirates.

Connie Mack always maintained that his 1912 team was the best one he ever managed. "They had everything that year," Connie often said. "Skill and experience and confidence that comes with winning. But some of them got hurt and some were over-confident and some broke training. So they lost the pennant. But they learned their lesson that year and came back strong in 1913 and 1914."

The team that should have won in 1912 finished third behind the Red Sox and Washington, the runner-up. This was a long drawn-out, agonizing Series that went eight games (one was a tie) and produced the sloppiest play and the most errors, one of which was the famous "$30,000 muff." This costly error was made by Giant center fielder Fred Snodgrass when he inexplicably dropped an easy routine fly in the tenth inning of the deciding game and handed the World Championship to the Red Sox. (The $30,000 was the difference between the winning and the losing players' shares of the booty.)

Matty pitched his heart out but had no support and lost two games. He also hurled the 6–6 tie. The Giants, playing like sand-lotters, made seventeen errors, and the Red Sox almost matched them by booting fourteen — a butter-fingered record that has yet to be surpassed.

One fan who saw all the games and loved every Giant error was

Baseball fans swarm about a subway kiosk in Times Square, New York, to watch the Series of 1912 on a scoreboard from which this photo was taken.

Honey Fitzgerald, the mayor of Boston. He sported a stove-pipe hat and was the leader of a group of several hundred noisy Boston fans who called themselves the Royal Rooters. Five years after the Series, Honey Fitzgerald had a new grandson. They named him John Fitzgerald Kennedy.

The 1913 Series was a rubber match between the two leagues as well as one between the two pennant-winning managers, John McGraw and Connie Mack. The National League had rung up three straight Series victories in 1907, 1908, and 1909, and the American League had replied with three consecutive wins in 1910, 1911, and 1912. In addition, both McGraw and Mack had won one Series from the other. Now it was the Giants and the A's again — for the last time, incidentally.

There was not much to it. The A's won the title with ease, four games to one. The Series spelled the end of the rivalry between the two incomparable pitchers, Christy Mathewson and Gettysburg Eddie Plank, that had started years before when both were college students in Pennsylvania. They faced each other in the second game and Matty, as usual, won the laurels. The next time they met, in the fifth game, Eddie finally took one from his nemesis with a two-hitter, winning 3 to 1. That game wrapped up the Series for the Philadelphians.

CHAPTER 3

THE MIRACLE BRAVES

(1914–1916)

CONNIE MACK was riding high in the fall of 1914. His boys had just won their fourth pennant in five years and had three World Championships under their collective belt. His kid infielders — called the "$100,000 infield" by sports writers, an enormous amount for those days — had matured and were at their peak.

John (Stuffy) McInnis, the shortest of the lot, played first and hardly knew what an error was. (One year he played 152 full games and made but one error all season for a fielding average of .999.) Eddie Collins, a future Hall of Famer, was on second; Jack Barry of Holy Cross College played short; and Home Run Baker, who had hit .450 in the 1913 Series, was on third. The pitching staff was the best in the league and the outfield was reliable although nothing extraordinary. The team's power was in the infield. Eddie Collins of Columbia University was runner-up that season to Ty Cobb for the league batting championship. Eddie hit .344, Cobb .368 for his eighth consecutive batting title. The A's won the flag by a comfortable margin of eight and a half games.

The race was quite different in the National League. It centered around John McGraw's Giants and the Boston Braves, at whose helm was a most unusual and colorful manager.

He was George Tweedy Stallings, a swarthy, dark-eyed tyrant who was capable of furious tantrums on the field; away from it he was courteous and well-mannered. He was truly a split personality —

The third man, Dick Rudolph, was tiny as pitchers go and had to rely on his brains. He had a beautiful curve and his control was close to perfection. Dick could get a little piece of the plate almost every time he threw, and in spite of his slight build he had as much staying power as the other two.

Hank Gowdy, the hawk-nosed, lanky backstop who was to be the first major leaguer to enlist in the United States Army in World War I, did most of the catching. For years after his retirement from the game he liked to talk about the Big Three. "It was guts mainly," Hank used to say. "They had plenty of guts and they always got the ball over in a pinch."

They also got excellent advice from coach Fred Mitchell, who was a baseball rarity. He had played major-league ball on both ends of the battery. Starting as a pitcher, he had injured his arm and had become a catcher. Fred's pre-game sessions with the Braves' pitchers and catchers were of great value. He knew both positions as few men have known them.

Actually, the Braves were a ragtag outfit at the start of the 1914 season. The year before they had been way down in the league standings in club batting and fielding and there was no reason to believe that the Big Three would show much improvement over their 1913 records, which were: Tyler, 16–17; James, 6–10; Rudolph, 14–13.

The team was not even considered a first division possibility by the baseball forecasters, and they seemed to be right when the season got under way and the Braves kept going down, down, down. On the night of July 4 the Braves found themselves in last place, fifteen games behind the front-running Giants. By baseball tradition, the team on top on July 4 generally wins the pennant and the one in the cellar stays there. The Braves weren't paying attention to tradition that year.

George Stallings said on July 4: "My team is ready now. We are in good shape. Watch us go to the top." No one took him seriously except his own players. For some reason — it may have been Stallings' dynamic drive or Johnny Evers' never-say-die spirit, or both — the team caught fire and became a fighting, cohesive unit.

It did not happen immediately. On July 19 the Braves were still last, but by eleven games instead of fifteen. Hank Gowdy always said that the climb started shortly after the club played an exhibition game against the minor-league Toronto club on an off day and got their ears pinned back. "It hurt our pride," the catcher recalled. "No matter what you say, no big-league club likes to lose to a minor-league outfit, even if it's only an exhibition game. The pasting we took galled us. From that moment on we went straight up."

Once they started, there was no halting the Braves. From mid-July on when it counted most, the Big Three were at their magnificent best. Bill James won nineteen out of his last twenty games, Dick Rudolph put together a twelve-game winning streak, and Lefty Tyler was virtually unbeatable.

They took over first place on September 2 by winning a double-header from the Phillies while the Giants were dropping a game to the Dodgers. They did not hold it, however. They slipped to second place behind the Giants, then drew up even with them, and on September 8 went into first place to stay. From that point on they zoomed skyward like a rocket, winning the pennant by ten and a half games.

Baseball had never seen anything like it before. The team became the "Miracle Braves." Stallings was the "Miracle Man."

There was still the World Series to play, though, against the experienced Athletics, and that would be the real test. The odds-makers did not give the Braves a chance. It was too much to ask, they figured, to keep that momentum up right on through the Series. The Braves were not concerned by odds or by baseball dopesters. They knew that they would beat the A's. Little Herbie Moran who played in the Braves' outfield offered a perfect example of the team's spirit when the A's captain, Harry Davis, congratulated him after Boston had clinched the flag and said, "You boys did a fine job, Herbie. We should have a great Series."

"Harry," replied Herbie in complete sincerity, "I really don't think you fellows will win a single game."

In the opening game the weak-hitting Braves shelled Chief Bender off the mound and stole three bases, including a double steal, to win, 7 to 1. This was the first time in Series history that an Athletics' pitcher had been knocked out. Foxy Dick Rudolph was the winner. The Chief never pitched another game for Connie Mack.

The next three were close but the Braves took them all. Eddie Plank lost the second game, 1–0, to Bill James. In the third game Lefty Tyler pitched ten innings to a 4–4 deadlock and was removed in the eleventh for a pinch hitter. Then Bill James took the mound, having

Manager George Stallings of the 1914 Miracle Braves sits on the bench with his "Big Three" pitching staff. From left to right: Bill James, Manager Stallings, George Tyler, Dick Rudolph.

had one day of rest between games, and won it in the twelfth, 5 to 4. In the fourth and final contest Dick Rudolph wrapped it up, 3 to 1. For the first time in history the Series was over in four games. Stallings had called upon his Big Three pitchers and no others. Rudolph and James each won two games.

The records of that Series are revealing. They show the Braves hitting 'way above their heads and the batting stars of the A's far below their season averages. Hank Gowdy became the first player to hit over .500 in a Series, turning in a dazzling .545 (against .243 for the season). Evers was close to him with .438, while the diminutive Maranville hit .307.

In contrast were the puny-hitting A's, of whom great things were expected. Home Run Baker was high man with .250, and next to him was Eddie Collins with a weak .214. Stuffy McInnis made two hits for .143 (season average: .314) and Jack Barry was good for only .071.

What had happened? Chief Bender gave his reasons for the stunning defeat in an interview held in 1948. The occasion was the return of the National League flag to Boston after a lapse of thirty-four years.

"One thing was their pitching," recalled the Chief with clarity. "We had great batters, but all of them, Eddie Collins, Stuffy McInnis, Home Run Baker, Jack Barry, were inside hitters, pull hitters.

"Rudolph and James never gave them one ball on the inside to hit. They pitched away from our men and made us hit what they wanted, rather than what we wanted."

Warming up to his subject, the Chief went into what was undoubtedly the most important reason of all for the A's downfall. "Spirit," he said. "Team spirit. It is something you cannot buy and cannot learn. It is infectious, like a tonic. You don't know where it comes from when you have it and you don't know where it goes when you lose it. The Braves had that kind of spirit that year. It wasn't mere combativeness. It was confidence and determination mixed. And that is a hard nut to crack."

Two years after the Chief had spoken, in 1950 at the mid-century mark, the Associated Press conducted a poll of the sportswriters and sportscasters to choose the greatest sports upset of the first fifty years of the century. The performance of the Miracle Braves won hands down by a margin of 128 votes to 53.

Far worse for Athletic fans than the loss of the Series was what the future held in store for them. Connie Mack sold all his star players that winter to various clubs and so impoverished the A's in talent that they crashed to last place in one season and stayed there for seven years. Not until 1923 did they climb out of the dungeon and then only to seventh place. This was perhaps the mightiest fall in baseball history.

The Braves lost ground, too, but they did not tumble as far as the A's. Stallings' boys showed up at spring training quarters in 1915 well-fed and flabby from a winter of living high on their World Series money. Rabbit Maranville was limping a bit. During the off season he had taken a turn in vaudeville, and in an attempt to show an audience in Lewiston, Maine, how he had slid into second in a key Series play, the Rabbit started at the back of the stage, overslid the footlights, and landed in a drum in the orchestra pit, breaking his leg.

The Big Three had the best years of their careers in 1914. It was also Johnny Evers' last big season. The team was never the same again and there was not much that the Miracle Man could do. He saw them stumble to second place in 1915, then to third the following year, and from 1917 through 1920 to sixth and seventh. Stallings quit them at the end of the 1920 season. A few years later the intense manager suffered a heart attack and when his doctor asked him if there was any way he could account for it, Stallings gasped, "Bases on balls, you so-and-so, bases on balls."

All was not gloom in Boston because of the Braves' downfall. No sooner did they slip from glory than up came the Red Sox. The American Leaguers brought World Championships to Boston in three of the next four years (1915, 1916, and 1918). They may not have been as exciting as the flamboyant young Braves but they were good.

They had one of the finest outfields ever assembled in Tris Speaker, Duffy Lewis, and Harry Hooper, and they had an up-and-coming young left-handed pitcher with a blazing fast ball who was used as a pinch hitter now and then. That was Babe Ruth.

It was the Phillies who beat out the Braves in the National League race in 1915. They were not rated highly by critics of the game, but everyone agreed that their star pitcher, Grover Cleveland Alexander, was one of the best in baseball. A right-hander with the control of

Grover Cleveland Alexander, the Phillies' great right-hander, had a 31–10 won-lost season in 1915, when he pitched against the Red Sox in the Series and won the opener.

Mathewson, Alex set up a string of National League pitching records year after year. Annually he would lead the league in such performances as: most strikeouts, lowest earned-run averages, most complete games, most shutouts, most games won. Alex was ready for the Red Sox when the teams met in the Series opener in Philadelphia on October 9. He had just completed a 31–10 season.

The Phillies won it, 3 to 1, and thereby established an unenviable record. It was the only World Series game they ever won. (In their next Series appearance thirty-five years later, the Yankees beat them four straight.) Something else worthy of mention happened in that game. It marked the first appearance of Babe Ruth in World Series play. In the ninth inning he was sent in to pinch hit for the Red Sox hurler, Ernie Shore. The Big Fellow sent a screamer down the first base line, but it was stabbed by Fred Luderus at first, who made an unassisted putout.

There was a bit of history made in the second game, too, but not on the field. In the stands on October 10 were President Woodrow Wilson and Mrs. Edith Galt, his wife-to-be. It was the first time a President of the United States attended a Series game. He did the honors by tossing out the first ball.

Oddly, that game and the two following it, both of which were played in Boston, ended with identical scores. The Red Sox won all three games, 2 to 1. A crowd of 42,000 witnessed the third game, which until then was the largest throng ever to see a Series game.

Almost every Series produces a hero and a goat. Duffy Lewis was the hero of the 1915 Series with his .444 batting average and several breath-taking catches in left field. The goat of the Series was not a player, but was the owner of the Phillies, Bill Baker. Baker had extra seats erected in front of the outfield stands so that he could squeeze in a few more fans. The field boxes shortened the already short outfield, making home runs much more possible.

In the fifth game, played in Philadelphia, the Red Sox were behind time and again, but they pulled the game out of the fire with home runs hit into the temporary stands. Duffy Lewis made one, Harry Hooper hit two, and the Sox won, 5 to 4. Their homers ended the Series and Baker lost out on the unplayed sixth game scheduled for Boston where the gate would have been about $80,000. Baker picked up a few hundred dollars with the extra seats but lost thousands because of them.

President Woodrow Wilson tossed out the ball to start the 1915 Series between the Red Sox and the Phillies. He was the first President to attend a World Series game.

The Red Sox topped the league again in 1916 but the Phillies failed to repeat despite the superb pitching of their ace, Alexander. He won thirty-three games, sixteen of which were shutouts for a big-league record. The Dodgers, who had not yet been graced with the nickname of Bums, took the National League flag.

Joy enveloped Boston for the third consecutive year as the Red Sox brought home the World Championship with the loss of only one game. Their single defeat was suffered at the hands of Colby Jack Coombs, the former Athletic pitcher who had been sold to the Dodgers. Jack beat the Red Sox in the third game, 4 to 3, to become the only pitcher in history to win World Series games in both leagues. (He had won Series games for the A's in 1910 and 1911.)

Duffy Lewis again distinguished himself with his bat and led his teammates with a batting average of .353. This is the only time that the same batter has led his club in two straight World Series. Duffy was topped, however, by the Dodgers' right fielder, Charles Dillon Stengel, known as Casey, who hit .364 against the Red Sox.

Babe Ruth was an outstanding American League pitcher that year with a 23–12 season record and was the low earned-run man with 1.75. He was a great favorite of the Boston fans, who thronged Fenway Park whenever he was scheduled to pitch. They did not think of him as a slugger, although he occasionally played the outfield. After all, his batting average for the season was a not-too-exciting .272.

The Babe turned in a notable performance in Boston in the second game of the Series, his only appearance. Opposing him was Sherry Smith, another southpaw. In the first inning Hi Myers, the Brooklyn center fielder, got hold of one of Ruth's fast ones for an inside-the-park homer. The Sox tied it up in the third, 1–1, and from then on it was a marathon pitching duel. Inning after inning the two southpaws took the mound and neither yielded a run. At last, in the fourteenth inning, when it was almost dark, the Red Sox put across the winning run. It is the longest game in Series history.

Ruth always took more pride in that single performance than in any of his countless home run records. That contest, incidentally, was the beginning of a Series record of consecutive scoreless innings by a pitcher. Ruth went on to pitch twenty-nine and two-thirds innings in a row before he gave up a run, a record that stood until 1961 when it was toppled by the Yankees' Whitey Ford.

A brief glance at the 1916 A's is in order here, if only to point out how violent the baseball fates can be. The club that had won the pennant two years before, compiled in 1916 the worst record ever known, with the loss of 117 games against thirty-six won. Tom Sheehan, who was one of the pitchers and is now a scout for the San Francisco Giants, often gabs about the season of misery. "I won one game that year and lost seventeen," he recalls with almost a touch of pride in his voice. "You think that's bad? Johnny Nabors won one and lost twenty, nineteen of them in a row. Elmer Myers and Bullet Joe Bush each lost twenty-four games. Together, we four pitchers lost eighty-five games. The club lost twenty in a row at one point. "We were so bad," smiles Sheehan, "that we came close to killing baseball."

CHAPTER 4

THE BLACK SOX

(1917–1919)

FROM TIME TO TIME there has appeared in sports books and magazines a tabulation of some of the outstanding events of World Series history, such as the "Ten Greatest Games," "Great Catches of the Series," "Game Winning Plays," and so on. No one, however, has ever suggested the subject, "Outstanding Bonehead Plays." If such a list were drawn up it would surely be headed by an astounding goof that took place in New York on October 15, 1917, in the sixth and final game of the Series between the Giants and the Chicago White Sox.

There was no scoring in the first three innings. Eddie Collins, the world's best second baseman, whom Connie Mack had sold to the White Sox, opened the fourth with a grounder to Heinie Zimmerman, the Giant third baseman. It was an ordinary roller, but Heinie threw wide past Walter Holke, on first, for a two-base error. Collins went to second. Davey Robertson in right field made things worse for the Giants a moment later when he dropped an easy fly hit by Joe Jackson, Chicago's great left fielder. That put Eddie Collins on third. Two miscues in a row like that would discourage most pitchers, but Rube Benton, on the mound for the Giants, remained steadfast even though the hard-hitting Hap Felsch was at bat. He induced Felsch to bounce a grounder back to him. Benton fielded it cleanly, quickly saw that Eddie Collins was way off third, and threw the ball to Zimmerman, thereby trapping Collins between third and home.

Collins was now a dead duck by all standards of big-league play.

45

The only thing he could do was to dance back and forth between third and home, delaying the inevitable tag-out as long as possible so that Jackson and Felsch could meanwhile advance to third and second.

Eddie jockeyed up and down. Catcher Bill Rariden with the ball came toward Eddie, then threw to Zimmerman. Suddenly Eddie saw that home plate was left unguarded and he dashed by the catcher. Right behind him ran Zimmerman with the ball in his hand, his arm extended in a desperate attempt to tag Eddie. The pair ran all the way down the base line in a hare-and-hound race and crossed the plate, one-two, Zimmerman still holding the ball with arm outstretched. It was a ridiculous sight and one that made McGraw fume to the point of near apoplexy. To make matters worse, a moment later Chick Gandil, Chicago's first baseman, came to bat and rapped out a long single, which brought home Jackson and Felsch. Those three runs were all the White Sox needed to win the game and the Series, although they scored one more run in the ninth for a 4–2 victory.

Whose fault was this boner of boners? Many critics have blamed Heinie Zimmerman, who became known as the "Man Who Chased Eddie Collins Across the Plate." Heinie always raged at what he believed — and many agreed with him — was a gross injustice.

"What was I supposed to do with the ball, eat it? There wasn't anybody to throw it to except Klem," was Heinie's answer. (Bill Klem was the plate umpire that day.) The blame must be shared by pitcher Rube Benton and Walter Holke, the first baseman. Neither of them covered the plate to back up their catcher. They were just standing around, fascinated.

This was McGraw's fourth straight World Series loss. Nevertheless, he was by all accounts one of the game's greatest managers. He piloted the Giants for thirty seasons and was only three times out of the first division. He won ten pennants and finished second ten times. Hard luck seemed to pursue him in the Series, however. He won but three World Championships in nine attempts.*

The scene switched back to Boston in 1918, a war year. The majors were ordered by Draft Director General Crowder to end the season on Labor Day or all players would be subject to the government's "Work or Fight" edict. An extra fifteen days were allowed them so that the Red Sox and the Cubs could play for the World Championship.

* McGraw's Giants won ten pennants but engaged in only nine World Series.

As Series go, this one was on the drab side in play as well as in attendance. Babe Ruth pitched the first game and won, 1–0, extending his scoreless innings string to twenty-two, then added seven more goose eggs to it in the fourth game, which he won, 3 to 2. His World Series pitching record is almost flawless and serves to support the contention of numerous baseball experts who maintain that if he had remained a pitcher he would undoubtedly have been one of the finest of all. In his two Series appearances as a pitcher, he won three games and lost none. He allowed only three runs in the thirty-one innings he pitched for an earned-run average of 0.87, or less than one run per nine innings. Ed Barrow, then manager of the Red Sox, recognized his devastating power at the plate and took him off the mound so that he could play him every day.

Babe was not the hero of the Series, however. Here again an unknown stole the show, in the person of George Whiteman, a run-of-the-mill outfielder the Red Sox had picked up from Toronto in mid-season of 1918. Had there not been a war on and a consequent shortage of players, George would never have seen the majors. He was thirty-six years old and had been knocking around in the minors for years. He didn't do much for Boston that season, hitting a mediocre .267.

Then came the set-to with the Cubs and for reasons beyond understanding, George went out and had a spectacular Series. He figured in *every* scoring inning the Red Sox had in six games and saved three victories with acrobatic catches. Here is a brief summary of his exploits:

In Game No. 1, George was the difference on two crucial plays. His single put the only run of the game in scoring position and he saved the game with a circus catch. That stab, incidentally, preserved Babe's scoreless innings streak.

In Game No. 2, Boston was blanked until the ninth when George tripled in the lone Red Sox run. The Cubs won, 3 to 1.

In Game No. 3, George drove in both runs for Boston's 2–1 victory, then robbed Dode Paskert of a homer with a diving catch against the wall.

In Game No. 4, George was one of the two Red Sox on base when Ruth hit a game-winning triple in a 3–2 battle.

In Game No. 5, George and all the Red Sox players had an off day. The Cubs blanked them, 3–0.

In Game No. 6, George reached his peak. His slashing drive in the third inning sent in all the runs the Red Sox needed to win, 2–1, but to make victory certain he made another spectacular catch to cut short a Cub rally in the eighth.

George could probably have defeated Honey Fitzgerald for mayor of Boston in the fall of 1918. He was the people's choice. Came 1919 and where was George? Back in Toronto.

A new rule passed by the National Commission in 1918 gave members of other first-division teams a share of the World Series money from the first four games. (This rule, incidentally, is in effect today.) It did not sit well with the contending teams of 1918, however, when they realized that their shares would be reduced, not only by the first-division distribution but also because gate receipts were running far behind average.

The players of both clubs got together before the fifth game in Boston and announced that they would strike unless they were guaranteed a $1,500 share for the winners and a $1,000 share for the losers. While the Red Sox and Cubs sulked in their dressing rooms and a crowd of 24,694 in the stands waited for more than an hour beyond the scheduled starting time, Ban Johnson, the American League founder and president, stormed into the players' quarters and gave them a tongue lashing. He told them, in effect, that they could either play or starve to death.

As it turned out, they came close to doing both. Individually, the winning Red Sox received about $1,100, which was not to be compared with any previous earnings of recent World Champions. Each Cub player netted around $600.

Attendance at the final game dipped to 15,238, the lowest figure since 1909. The faithful Boston fans who made up the crowd saw what was to be the last Red Sox Series game in more than a quarter of a century.

Many sound baseball men consider the 1919 White Sox the best all-round team ever to take the field. It was a team of stars, of great hitters, defensive players, and superb pitchers, a team that had everything, including a bunch of rough, tough boys and a sprinkling of gentlemen. It was a team of dissension, of player cliques, and it seethed with bitterness and discord. Harmony, spirit, and cooperation are held to be essential in a great team. The White Sox had none of these qualities. Yet they were so good that they won going away. They were simply unstoppable — and they were one more thing: they were crooked. Eight of them were, at any rate, and they came very close to wrecking baseball as our national pastime. Fate found a perfect name for this team. By merely changing "White" to "Black" the team became the Black Sox, a nickname that clings to it today and will never be forgotten.

This was virtually the same club that, playing on the level, had won the 1917 Series against the Giants. The following year much of their power was shorn by draft and enlistment and they skidded in the pennant race. Under the leadership of William J. (Kid) Gleason, a peppery ex-Oriole, they came back strong in 1919 and were considered a cinch to take the Series from the Cincinnati Reds, champions of the older league.

One of the White Sox super-stars was "Shoeless" Joe Jackson, so called because as a youngster he once played a game for a southern club in his stocking feet to spare a sore heel. Shoeless Joe was an illiterate country boy but he was close to Cobb as a hitter and he had an arm like a gun. In 1911 in his first full season he hit .408 (for Cleveland), but failed to win the league batting title because of Cobb's unbelievable .420 average. Joe was never below .300. He roamed left field next to Hap Felsch, who was one of the best defensive outfielders.

Ray Schalk, a one-man catching staff, was without peer as a backstop. Pitcher Eddie Cicotte (29–7), master of a trick delivery known as the shine ball, was outstanding, as were the other moundsmen, Claude Williams (23–11) and Red Faber, winner of three Series games in 1917. On first was tough Chick Gandil, a fine fielder and also the club's trouble-maker, who was to be the key man in the scandal. Honest Eddie Collins was on second, Swede Risberg, who had a wonderful arm, played short, and scrappy and aggressive Buck Weaver was the game's top third baseman. Utility infielder Fred McMullin, who had scouted the Reds before the Series, was one of the conspirators.

The fix was first discussed mid-season in a New York hotel when the ringleaders, Eddie Cicotte, Chick Gandil, and Claude Williams met a group of gamblers and discussed terms. The three White Sox named five other players who they thought should be taken into the plot to make certain that it would go through. They were: Swede Risberg, Joe Jackson, Hap Felsch, Fred McMullin, and Buck Weaver. All agreed to go along, with the exception of Buck Weaver. He attended two meetings and knew that the fix was on, but he remained silent about it, to his everlasting regret.

The gamblers promised the players $100,000. It seems incredible today that such a sum could buy almost an entire team to throw the country's greatest sports event. It was a sizable sum, however, in view of the average salary then paid to the game's acknowledged stars, which was about $6,000. Besides, these men were chronic malcontents and they despised the White Sox owner, Charles Comiskey, who was known as the tightest owner in baseball. He paid the lowest salaries in the majors, a fact that made the conspirators an easy target for the gamblers.

A few days before the Series started, the White Sox were the established odds-on-favorites by a lopsided 3 to 1. Then the sure-thing gamblers began betting on the Reds and were soon covering everything in sight at the juicy odds. The avalanche of Cincinnati money caused the odds to switch the other way, making the Reds the 8-to-5 choice before the first game. Surely something was fishy. The Reds were not in the same class with the White Sox as a ball club. Something queer was going on. So said sporting men everywhere, as well as baseball writers and the gamblers who were not in on the fix but sensed it. Ugly rumors flooded hotel lobbies and bars.

The fix was on, all right. The agreed-upon signal for the gambling group, who did not trust the ball players, was for the White Sox pitcher in the first game to hit the first batter. The play would be flashed all over the country on the play-by-play telegraph wires and the gamblers would immediately get into action with more bets.

Eddie Cicotte, the master of control, threw the key ball and Maurice Rath, Cincinnati's first batter, took it right between the shoulder blades. Eddie had carried out his role to perfection. By the fourth inning Cicotte was out of there and the White Sox were out of the ball game. The Reds won it, 9 to 1. Catcher Ray Schalk kept shaking his head in the clubhouse after the game. He could not understand why Cicotte had repeatedly crossed up his signals.

Claude Williams started the second game for the White Sox. He obliged the gamblers by walking three men in one inning, something he hadn't done all year, and gave up two hits. The Reds got three

A crooked pitcher with payoff money in his hip pocket is the way this cartoonist saw the National Pastime when it was revealed that the 1919 World Series had been fixed.

runs, one more than they needed. The White Sox lost, 4–2. They had managed to score just three runs in two games.

Kid Gleason knew that something was wrong, especially after Ray Schalk told him that he had never seen Williams pitch that way. "I'd call for one high and outside and I'd get it in the dirt," said the puzzled catcher.

Kid Gleason told Comiskey of his suspicions and the White Sox owner repeated them to John Heydler, president of the National league, on the train going to Chicago. (The first two games had been played in Cincinnati.) Heydler aroused Ban Johnson who was asleep in his compartment — it was then around 3 A.M. — and told him what Comiskey had said. "That's the yelp of a beaten cur," said Johnson, who despised Comiskey and was, in fact, not speaking to him because of a personal feud.

Something else was wrong besides the thrown ball games. The gamblers were not paying off the players as they had promised. They had paid an initial installment of $10,000 before the Series started and they agreed to pay the rest in installments after each game, but they were not making these payments. They gave an evasive excuses to the players and promised to pay in full later. They never did, though.

It has never been clear whether the conspirators were infuriated by the non-payoff and really tried to win or whether it was Dickie Kerr's masterful pitching that won the third game for the White Sox. At any rate, the pint-sized Kerr was on the level and he allowed only three hits to bring the Sox their first win, 3 to 0.

Eddie Cicotte was his crooked self the next day. In the fifth inning he fielded an easy roller and threw the ball into the stands. Later in the same inning he let a run come in by stabbing at Joe Jackson's perfect throw from left field to the plate and deflecting the ball from its course. Cicotte's two errors gave the Reds their two runs for a 2–0 victory.

The Sox were now behind three games to one, but they would have to drop two more in order to lose the championship, as this was a five-games-out-of-nine Series. It had been lengthened from the previous four-games-out-of-seven by the National Commission. The best-of-nine system was tried for three years (1919, 1920, 1921) but it proved to be too long to maintain public interest.

The White Sox took their fourth loss, a 5–0 shutout, at the hands of a shine-ball artist, Hod Eller, who struck out six men in a row. They were now within one game of dumping the Series. The diminutive Dickie Kerr kept them alive, however, with an honest 5–4 win.

Eddie Cicotte pleaded with Kid Gleason for another chance at the Reds. There was such a sincere tone in his voice that Gleason decided to let him start. For the first time in the Series Cicotte was himself and pitched a winning game. Just why he did so has never been explained. Perhaps it was because the fixed players had not been paid what they had been promised and they were really trying to win. Whatever the reason, the Sox won, 4 to 1. The end came a day later when Claude Williams got shelled for four runs in the first inning and the Reds went on to win, 10 to 5.

The Series broke all previous records in total receipts and attendance and reached new highs in players' shares. The Reds were the first to go through the $5,000 mark, each player receiving $5,207.01. The White Sox, crooked and honest alike, were each paid $3,254.36. The games went into the record book, the players went home, and baseball dopesters wrote thousands of words about the stunning upset. The winter passed, the 1920 season got under way, and the White Sox, again heavily favored to win the flag, found themselves in a three-cornered race with the Cleveland Indians and Yankees.

The lid didn't blow off until the middle of September, when evidence came to light that the Series had been fixed. Abe Attell, the ex-featherweight champion, admitted that he had a leading hand in the deal and named the players. The *Chicago Tribune* displayed an open letter on the front page of the sports section, demanding that the Chicago Grand Jury investigate the Series. So far the players had admitted nothing.

On the morning of September 28, 1920, Kid Gleason went to Comiskey and said, "Boss, do you want the truth? I think I can get it for you. Cicotte is about to break down." The pitcher was taken to the office of Comiskey's lawyer and he at once broke into tears and told all. Later, before the Grand Jury, he again confessed, as did Jackson, Williams, and Felsch.

After the four players gave the details, Comiskey immediately suspended all eight. This was followed months later by criminal prosecutions against them by the State of Illinois, but a trial jury acquitted them. The state's case had been weakened by the mysterious disappearance of the signed confessions, which the conspirators now repudiated.

The players were jubilant. The same night the verdict was handed down, the eight Black Sox and the jury that had acquitted them shamefully got together and celebrated a "victory party" in a Chicago restaurant. Technically they were entitled to reinstatement on the White Sox club.

They did not reckon with Judge Kenesaw Mountain Landis, however, the newly appointed Commissioner of Baseball, who replaced the National Commission to become the one-man ruling czar of organized baseball. The Judge quickly killed any hopes the players had of getting back into the game. In a statement issued immediately after the acquittal, he said:

"Regardless of the verdict of juries, no player that throws a ball game, no player that entertains proposals or promises to throw a game, no player that sits in a conference with a bunch of crooked players and gamblers where the ways and means of throwing games are discussed, and does not promptly tell his club about it, will ever again play professional baseball."

For many years thereafter attempts were made to have some of the players restored to good standing. Many fans felt that Buck Weaver had been given harsh treatment. True, he never saw a cent of crooked money and he played his best in the Series, hitting .324. Nevertheless, he knew of the crooked deal and he did nothing to prevent it. One year a petition signed by 10,000 fans asking for Weaver's reinstatement was sent to Judge Landis. He rejected it without comment.

Shoeless Joe had supporters also. He was, they said, an ignorant fellow, easy-going and good-natured, and he hardly knew what was going on. He didn't see any of the payoff money, either. So he said, at any rate. One thing in his favor was his Series record. He topped both clubs with a batting average of .375. How could he be crooked and hit that way? Perhaps it was because Joe, a natural hitter, just couldn't resist some of those fat pitches that were served up to him, and momentarily forgot all about the shady business.

Baseball kept a watchful eye on the eight. Long after the Series, when Shoeless Joe signed as a coach of a class D minor league club in Alabama, word came down from Commissioner Landis advising the club to get rid of him. It did in a hurry.

The name "Black Sox" forever followed the eight. Those who are alive still look back upon the deed with anguish and remorse. As recently as 1956 the once-tough ringleader, Chick Gandil, who worked as a plumber in California ever since the 1919 Series, wrote:

"About this time each year when people start getting excited about the World Series, I find myself wanting to crawl into a cave. I think you'd feel the same if you had the memories I do."

Eddie Cicotte, a topnotch pitcher, confessed that he had accepted money from gamblers to throw games in the 1919 Series. Cicotte and seven other White Sox players were barred from baseball for life. Judge Kenesaw Mountain Landis was appointed Baseball Commissioner following the fixed Series of 1919. He banished the crooked players and helped restore public confidence in the game.

For some time after the scandal broke, the structure of baseball was in serious danger of collapsing. Thousands of fans quit the game in disgust. Public confidence was badly shaken. It was restored in part by the quick and severe punishment meted out to the offending players. Fans began to realize that baseball was making a sincere effort to clean its own house and would not tolerate any funny business in any form. The fiery Landis made that clear to the club owners and also hammered home the message to the American public.

Another thing that helped save the game was the rise to fame of Babe Ruth, the game's most glamorous and colorful figure as well as its greatest slugger. The Babe's fabulous feats on the diamond did much to dim the memory of the unsavory ones. Just as they made their exit, the Babe burst upon the scene to become the greatest gate attraction the game has ever known. The right man had come along at the right time.

Babe Ruth, the game's greatest slugger and its Number One gate attraction, appeared upon the scene when baseball was at a low ebb in public esteem. He made the turnstiles whirl again.

CHAPTER 5

THE RISE OF THE YANKEES

(1920–1928)

WHEN THE SCANDAL bomb exploded in September, 1920, and the traitors were suspended, the White Sox staggered down the stretch with a makeshift team and lost the pennant to the Cleveland Indians by two games. The Indians were led by the incomparable Tris Speaker, who performed his managerial duties efficiently and at the same time played 150 games and batted .388. Speaker, who played the shallowest center field ever seen and could travel back farther than any man, was a demon at the plate, as his lifetime mark of .344 makes plain. Invariably he is chosen by baseball experts for a place on the mythical all-time greatest outfield along with Cobb and Ruth. No other outfielder besides these three has ever been considered for a place.

In the National League the Brooklyn Dodgers were the surprise winners. They took the flag with the identical team that had finished fifth the year before, twenty-seven games behind the Reds. How did they do it? No one could explain it then and no one has yet, except to say, "It could happen only in Brooklyn."

There were other things that fans were talking about besides the scandals as the 1920 Series approached. One was the tragic death of Ray Chapman, the Indians' dazzling shortstop and .300 hitter, who was at bat when he was struck on the left temple by a fast ball thrown by Yankee pitcher Carl Mays in a game played in New York on August 16. He keeled over and died a few hours later without regaining consciousness. The death of the popular Chapman shattered his teammates and they surrendered first place to the Yankees, but afterward bounded back.

Fans were also talking about Babe Ruth and he gave them plenty to talk about. The year before he had started things by blasting the unprecedented figure of twenty-nine home runs and had hit .322 for the Red Sox. Fans everywhere followed his climb up the home run ladder in 1919. In Boston he was idolized.

On January 9, 1920, a bombshell hit Boston in the form of an announcement that their darling, Babe Ruth, the new home run sensation, the most exciting player to come along in years, had been sold to the New York Yankees. The villain was Harry Frazee, a theatrical producer who had bought the Red Sox three years before and knew nothing about baseball. He needed money for a theatrical venture and sold the Babe to the Yankees for $125,000. Later he sold almost all his best players to New York and ruined the Red Sox for a generation.

In New York the Babe came into his own. He immediately captivated the city and was the center of attention wherever he went. There seemed to be no limit to his powers. In 1920, his first year as a Yankee, he hit fifty-four homers, batted .376, played first base and the outfield, and even pitched a few innings.

Fans were still talking about the Babe when they settled down to watch the Dodgers and the Indians in the Series of 1920. They saw a not-too-difficult victory for the Indians, who won, five games to two, and they saw a game that will be talked about as long as baseball is played.

This was the fifth game, played in Cleveland on October 10 when the Series was tied at two-all. Things began happening in the first inning when Elmer Smith, the Indians' right fielder, came to bat with three men on and hit a homer over the high right-field fence. It was the first grand-slam home run ever hit in Series play. In the third inning Jim Bagby, who was hurling for the Indians, contributed to the record book by poling out a homer in right center to become the first pitcher in Series history to make a four-base clout. At this point the Dodger pitcher was relieved by Clarence Mitchell, a southpaw spitballer, who was soon to make some Series history of his own.

It happened in the fifth inning. The Dodgers had two runners on base with none out when Mitchell came to the plate. The runners were

Pete Kilduff, who was on second, and Otto Miller, on first. Mitchell, a good hitter, took a full cut at one of Bagby's fast balls and hit a line drive. It looked like a double at least. Both base runners took off at the crack of the bat. Then suddenly up rose Bill Wambsganss, the Indians' second baseman, and speared the ball for out number one. Quickly he touched second, putting out Kilduff who was well on his way to third. Then Wambsganss tagged out the plodding Miller, who had run from first to second with his head down and knew not what was in store for him. In a flash Wambsganss had completed an un-assisted triple play, a feat that has yet to be duplicated in Series play. Just to make it a perfect day in reverse for Mitchell, the unfortunate fellow hit into a double play in his next time up.

In 1921 the incredible Ruth had another terrific season. The huge moon-faced slugger with top-heavy torso tapering down to a pair of skinny legs that made him look, as one sportswriter put it, "like a cone stuffed with too much ice cream," clouted fifty-nine homers, batted in 170 runs, and hit .378. Despite his weird dimensions and often overfed stomach, the Babe was a graceful outfielder and had an excellent arm. He could run, too. In 1921 he stole seventeen bases.

It is doubtful if any ball player had so much to do with the swift rise of a team as did Ruth with the Yankees. They won their first pennant in 1921 and followed it up with two more in succession. The three-year string was the foundation on which the Yankees built what was to become the greatest and most successful baseball organization in the world.

At the same time the National League scene was dominated by John McGraw and his snappy, aggressive Giants. They outdid the Yankees by putting together a four-year string of pennants. This was the brightest era the Giants have ever known and it saw McGraw reach his highest peak as a manager. The short, gray-haired tyrant, who was known as "Little Napoleon," was still a die-hard National Leaguer. He still looked upon the other league with contempt and could not even find anything good to say about Babe Ruth. "We will pitch to him the same as we would anyone else," said McGraw just before the Series.

The 1921 event was the last of the five-out-of-nine set and all the games were played at the Polo Grounds, with the clubs alternating daily in the role of the home team. (The Yankees were then tenants of the Polo Grounds, having been forced to give up their own ball park in 1913. The present Yankee Stadium had not then been built.) It was the first one-city Series since the White Sox and the Cubs fought it out back in 1906. Sportswriters called this three-year cluster the Subway Series.

The key men in McGraw's lineup were Long George Kelly on first, Dave (Beauty) Bancroft at short, and Frankie Frisch, who had come from Fordham University directly to the Giants and was a star from the beginning. Frisch played third, sometimes second. The Giants had a fine outfield in Georgie Burns, Ross Youngs, and Irish Meusel whose brother, Bob, played right field for the Yankees. The pitching staff was strong. The Yankees, managed by the tiny Miller Huggins, got off to a galloping start by taking the first two games by the identical scores of 3–0. Up to this time no team had ever won a Series after losing the first two games, and defeat looked more certain than ever in the third game when the Yankees knocked out Giant pitcher Fred Toney in the third inning and put four runs across. The Babe banged in two of the runs and now it was 4–0 for the Yankees and the Giants had yet to score a run in the Series.

But the tide turned rapidly and dramatically. Back came the Giants with four runs in their half of the third. They broke the deadlock in the eighth inning with eight more runs and won, 13 to 5. They won the next game, dropped the fifth, and then took three in a row for the title, five games to three. It was McGraw's first World Championship since 1905. The Babe topped his teammates with a .313 average, but his absence in the final games because of an arm injury undoubtedly hurt their chances. The often repeated phrase of the Ruthian Era, "As Ruth goes, so go the Yankees," was coined at this time.

As a perfect example of how true that phrase was, consider what happened to Ruth and to the Yankees in the 1922 Series. The Babe was a complete flop. In seventeen times at bat he touched the Giants for only two hits, a single and a double, for a humiliating average of .118. The Yankees sank with him. They did not win a game. For the first and only time in their history, they were shut out without a single victory in a World Series. There was a ten-inning 3–3 tie in the second game, called because of darkness, but that was as close at the Yankees came to winning. As Ruth went to .118 so did the other Yankees go: shortstop Everett Scott to .143, catcher Wally Schang to .188, center fielder Whitey Witt to .222, and so on. Bob Meusel with an even .300 was the only Yankee in the select circle.

The Giants walloped the ball all over the Polo Grounds, the way the Yankees were supposed to hit it. Among the Giant regulars Heinie Groh, the squat third baseman who used a freak bottle-shaped bat, hit .474; Frisch, with years of greatness ahead of him, batted .471; Youngs hit .375; and catcher Frank Snyder turned in .333. The club as a whole averaged .309, a National League Series record, while the Yankees were held to .203, or more than 100 points below the champions. Although McGraw was to produce two more pennant winners, the 1922 aggregation was his last truly great team.

McGraw should have been the happiest of managers after spanking the Yankees two years in a row, but he wasn't. He was troubled and bitter. During the 1921 and 1922 seasons he had seen the Yankees outdraw the Giants in the Polo Grounds. The humiliating box office figures meant that the Giants were a secondary attraction in their own park. It was the Babe, of course, who was drawing the crowds, but McGraw saw the whole Yankee club as a threat. "The Yankees are getting too powerful," he warned Charles Stoneham, the Giants' owner. "We can't afford to let them play in the Polo Grounds any longer. If we kick them out, they won't be able to find another location on Manhattan Island. They'll have to move to the Bronx or Long Island. The fans will forget about them and they'll be through."

Much as landlord Stoneham disliked losing the rent money, he requested the Yankees to leave. "As quickly as possible," he told Yankee owner, Jake Ruppert. It turned out to be the most costly eviction notice in the history of baseball. The Yankees bought a site in the Bronx, just across the river from the Polo Grounds, and Ruppert built baseball's biggest park, Yankee Stadium.

The Babe dedicated the new park on April 18, 1923, in traditional Ruthian fashion by slugging a three-run homer, and the Yankees whipped the Red Sox, 4 to 1, before a capacity house of some 60,000 people, the largest crowd that had ever seen a ball game. Most of them had followed the Yankees across the river to the Bronx, contrary to McGraw's prediction.

This photo shows the first game played in Yankee Stadium, on April 18, 1923, when the Yankees battled the Red Sox in the season's opener. Babe Ruth rose to the occasion, as usual, by hitting a game-winning homer.

Ruth had another great season in 1923, although he did not smash any home run records. He batted .393, the highest mark of his career, but it wasn't good enough to win the league title, as Harry Heilmann, the Detroit powerhouse, batted .403. The Babe led the league in homers with forty-one and shared with Tris Speaker the runs-batted-in honors with 130. The baseball scribes of the nation voted him the "American League's Greatest All-Round Player" of 1923.

The Yankees, as usual, rose with him and finished sixteen games in front of second-place Detroit. It was the same ball club that had been such a dismal failure against the Giants the year before except for the addition of pitcher Herb Pennock, a splendid left-hander who had been bought from Boston.

In the fall the Yankees staged a house-warming for the Giants in their new Stadium and crushed them, four games to two. The Babe, running on high, socked three homers and hit .368 for the Series. Spectacular as the Babe's performance was, the talk of the Series was the Giants' center fielder, a 33-year-old clown nearing the end of his career, whose name was Casey Stengel. He alone gave the Giants their only two wins.

In the ninth inning of the first game at Yankee Stadium, with the score tied at 4–4, Casey hit an inside-the-park homer, which he completed on one shoe, grinning as he ran and slid into the plate. It gave the Giants a 5–4 victory.

In the seventh inning of the so-far scoreless third game, Casey hit a mighty one into the Stadium's right field bleachers, much to the astonishment of himself, the Yankees, and his teammates. Earlier, the Yankee bench had been riding him hard about his "lucky" first-game homer.

As he made his triumphal tour of the bases, Casey thumbed his nose at the Yankee dugout all the way around. It was the only run of the ball game. Jake Ruppert, outraged at Casey's ungenteel conduct, rushed to the box occupied by Judge Landis and demanded loudly that the Baseball Commissioner discipline Stengel. Landis looked the owner of the Yankees in the eye and said: "No. When a man hits a home run in a World Series game he should be permitted some exuberance — particularly when his name is Casey Stengel."

If it had not been for Casey the Yankees would have won the Series in four straight games. As a reward to him, McGraw sold him to the lowly Braves a few weeks later. "Well, maybe I'm lucky," grinned Casey when he got the news. "If I'd hit three homers, McGraw might have sent me out of the country."

The first Series to be played at Yankee Stadium produced the first million-dollar gate and set a new attendance record of 301,430. It was also the first Series to be broadcast (by the late Graham McNamee). It was the Yankees' first World Championship and they have been the Big Team in the Big Park in the Big Town ever since. That was the start.

Their rise to power and almost complete dominance of the American League did not come without a setback or two, however. There was, in fact, a falling off the very next year due to overconfidence, complacency, and the inevitable letdown after a string of triumphs. The slogan, "As Ruth goes . . ." for once did not work in 1924. The Big Fellow had another banner season, hitting .378 to lead the league in batting for the first and only time in his career, but he could not pull the Yankees out of second place, which is where they finished.

A standard gag that kept making the rounds of the vaudeville houses in those days went something like this:

"Washington!" the stage comic would say. "Washington! First in war, first in peace — and last in the American League. Ha, ha, ha, ha!"

It got a laugh everywhere except in Washington, where the Senators were very often a last-place club and hardly ever in the first division. During this long bleak period, however, the Senators were graced by the presence of one of the game's finest men and perhaps its greatest pitcher.

He was Walter Perry Johnson, a shy and gentle right-hander who could throw a baseball with the speed of a bullet. In the days of trick deliveries, he never "doctored" the ball. He just reared back and threw it without making the slightest attempt to conceal anything. Every batter knew what was coming — a fast ball. They knew, too, that Johnson had beautiful control and would never throw a duster or a bean ball. Yet they could not hit him, so terrific was his speed. One baseball critic said of him: "He was the greatest pitcher who ever lived despite the fact that everybody in the park knew what he was going to throw." The modest and unassuming Johnson was the game's most beloved figure.

He pitched twenty-one consecutive years for Washington. With atrocious teams behind him most of the time, he won 413 games. Only one other pitcher ever won more than 400 games — Cy Young, who had 510 to his credit, most of which were won in the 1890's. No modern pitcher is anywhere near Johnson in games won. Never until the twilight of his career in 1924, in his eighteenth season with the Senators, did he have the opportunity to pitch in a World Series. It was Washington's first flag in history.

The Giants were expected to win in 1924, but the Senators were the sentimental favorites because Walter Johnson was getting his chance at last. It was Bucky Harris, the popular "Boy Manager" of

Walter Johnson, who threw the fastest ball ever seen, pitched twenty-one consecutive years for Washington and won 413 games. Many experts rate him the greatest pitcher who ever lived.

the Senators (he was 27), against veteran John McGraw. President Calvin Coolidge and his wife attended the opener in Washington's Griffith Stadium, with 5,000 temporary seats added.

It was a see-saw, exciting Series with each club winning and losing games in turn. Washington fans wept openly when Walter Johnson lost the first one, a twelve-inning heart-breaker. He went all the way. In his next appearance, in the fifth game at the Polo Grounds, there were more tears — in the press box this time, shed by hardened baseball writers — when poor Walter fell apart and the Giants won, 6–2.

The Senators won the sixth game and the Series came down to the final contest with the teams at three games each. It turned out to be one of baseball's unforgettable games that left the Washington crowd of 31,667 fans exhausted and limp.

The Boy Manager started things in the fourth inning when he made his team's first hit, a homer into the temporary stands. Two innings later the Senators got the jitters and the Giants gained a 3-to-1 advantage. Things looked bad for Washington until the eighth when the Senators got two men on base, one of whom was a pinch hitter for pitcher Fred Marberry. The key hit came off the bat of the Boy Manager who knocked a grounder down the third-base line to Freddy Lindstrom. The ball suddenly hopped over Freddy's head for a single and two runs came in.

With the game tied 3–3 when Washington took the field in the ninth, the crowd began shouting, "We want Johnson!" The roof of Griffith Stadium almost came off when their hero started moving to the mound. There was still a chance that he might win himself a World Series game. It did not look that way, though, as Johnson was constantly in hot water. But good support and his own great heart pulled him through time and again. In the twelfth the game was still deadlocked at 3–3. Then the gremlins began to work against the Giants.

As the Senators came to bat in the twelfth, catcher Muddy Ruel raised a pop foul behind the plate that should have been the second out, but Hank Gowdy somehow got his foot tangled up in his own mask and the ball thudded to earth. Given a reprieve, Muddy, who had yet to make a hit in the Series in twenty tries, smacked a double to left. Johnson batted for himself and got on through a Giant error. Then up came center fielder Earl McNeely, who hit a sharp bounder toward Freddy Lindstrom. It appeared to be an easy play — but wait! Again the ball took a funny bounce and hopped over Freddie's head into left field. Ruel scored and that was the Series.

Lindstrom, who was never one to make alibis, later said that the odd hops had been caused by pebbles around third. Many players agreed with him. Whatever the reason for the Giants' downfall, Mc-Graw could not help but state to the press: "The better team did not win."

On the train going back to New York the Giants were dazed at the outcome. Rube Bentley, one of the finer pitchers, made his team-mates feel a little better by saying, "Cheer up, boys. It just looks as though the Good Lord couldn't stand seeing Walter get beat again."

Bucky Harris' Senators clicked again in 1925. This was the year that the Yankees went into a violent tailspin. The Babe's after-dark activities and his constant battles with manager Huggins brought his batting average far below his 1924 pace. Huggins slapped him with a fine of $5,000, baseball's all-time high, and suspended him indefinitely. The team finished in seventh place. Never again were the Yankees to sink to such low estate.

First baseman Lou Gehrig was the most durable player in history. The Yankee powerhouse appeared in 2,130 consecutive games, a period that spanned fifteen seasons (1925–1939).

Rogers Hornsby, baseball's best right-hand hitter, batted over .400 three times and reached a peak of .424 in 1924. He managed the Cardinals when they whipped the Yankees in the 1926 World Series.

Tony Lazzeri, Yankee second baseman, goes down swinging with the bases loaded and two men out in the deciding game of the 1926 Series. Tony was struck out by the veteran Grover Cleveland Alexander.

It was the seventh inning and the Cards were ahead, 3–2, but the Yankees had loaded the bases with two out. Tony Lazzeri, a dangerous clutch hitter, was up. Old Pete studied his man for a moment and then let go. Tony swung and missed. Tony hit the next pitch on a line into the left field stands, a foul by two feet. Old Pete, unruffled as always, threw once more and Tony went down swinging. Alexander finished the game, holding the Yankees hitless to save the Cards' lead and win the World Championship. Later, Old Pete, remembering how near to a home run that foul of Lazzeri's had been, said of the famous episode: "A foot or two made the difference between being a hero and a bum."

If the Yankees were shaken by the close Series defeat, they showed no signs of it in 1927. They took first place on opening day and were never headed during the 174 days of the season. They drew so far out in front that it was no race at all. On Labor Day they clinched the pennant in Boston and went on to win a record of 110 games, finishing nineteen full games ahead of the second-place Athletics.

Was this the greatest of all teams? Many baseball historians think so and several newspaper polls indicate that it was. There is no doubt that it was the most awesome combination of hitting power, pitching talent, and general all-round ability. In addition, it had the priceless qualities that every great ball club must have: spirit, confidence, desire, and pride in its work.

What made the 1927 Yankees so outstanding was that almost every member of the team picked that season to have the best year of his life. The Babe hit his peak with sixty home runs and hit .356. Gehrig, who followed him in the batting order to form the most deadly one-two punch baseball has ever known, hit .373, poled out forty-seven homers, and batted in 175 runs. Center fielder Earle Combs, the leadoff man, hit .356, and Bob Meusel, the lightest hitter in the outfield, averaged .337. Tony Lazzeri, on second, hit .309. As a team they batted an unmatched .307 and scored nearly 1,000 runs during the season. No wonder the nickname "Murderers' Row" stuck to them forever.

Waite Hoyt, the schoolboy moundsman, had a 22–7 season and led a fine pitching staff which included Herb Pennock, George Pipgras, and Wilcey Moore.

There is not much to say about the 1927 Series. The Yankees were picked by everyone to beat the Pittsburgh Pirates, National League pennant winners, and they did just that — in four straight games. The Babe didn't have much time to get rolling in only four games, but he managed to hit two homers and he batted .400. It was the Yankees' first Series sweep, the first of many more to come.

It was still "Murderers' Row" in 1928, but the Yankees did not finish out of sight as they had the year before. They won the pennant, but only after a grueling struggle with the A's, a team that was at last coming to life again after years of despair. Beset by injuries as well as by complacency, the Yankees squeaked home with a margin of two and a half games over Connie Mack's boys.

In the older league it was the Cardinals again, who also had to stage a late-season drive to win the flag. They nosed out the Giants by two games. An important change had been made since they whipped the Yankees two years before. Frankie Frisch had succeeded Hornsby, the batting king, on second, and little Rabbit Maranville of the Miracle Braves of 1914 was at short. Old Pete, now 41, was still a winning pitcher, with a 16–9 season.

The 1928 Series was another breeze for the Yankees. Their sensational hitting shattered the Cards and gave them a revengeful four-straight victory. The Babe reached the absolute summit of his Series career. The Big Fellow murdered the Cardinal pitching for a record .625 average and duplicated his feat of the 1926 Series by again hitting three homers in a single game. Lou Gehrig, the man in the shadow of the mighty one, smacked four homers in the Series and hit .545. Old Pete took a beating in the second game, losing 9 to 3.

The Yankees had now won eight straight Series games. Would they never stop? Down in Philadelphia wise old Connie Mack had an idea that he could stop them — and he did.

The 1927 Yankee outfield, shown here, has never been equaled in hitting power. From left to right (with 1927 batting averages): Earle Combs, cf (.356), Babe Ruth, rf (.356), Bob Meusel, lf (.337).

CHAPTER 6

THE TWILIGHT OF THE A'S AND THE GAS HOUSE GANG

(1929–1935)

CONNIE MACK, at the age of 67 in 1929, had not won a flag for Philadelphia in fifteen years, not since the Miracle Braves had humbled him back in 1914. In the past few years, however, he had been collecting a powerhouse. In so doing, the shrewd Connie was adapting himself perfectly to the changes that were sweeping the national game.

The ball had been needled, for one thing, and the accent was now on hitting. The old school of baseball would no longer win pennants — the school of the old Orioles and of McGraw and of Connie himself in 1914, in the heyday of inside stuff, like the squeeze, the hit-and-run, and base stealing. Now it was the age of the big punch, the homer, the big inning, and Connie went right along with it.

The team's power centered around strong-boy Jimmy Foxx, who could play anywhere, Al Simmons, whose batting form was all wrong but who could knock the cover off the ball, and Mickey Cochrane, the game's best catcher who was a good enough hitter to bat third in the lineup, instead of in the customary eighth spot. The star pitcher was Lefty Grove, a speed-ball thrower and a great competitor. These four players, incidentally, are now in the Baseball Hall of Fame.

Jimmy Foxx, who finally found himself at first base after catching and playing third, was not far from the Babe as a home run hitter. He clouted fifty-eight one year and eventually totaled 534, more than

74

any other right-hander and second only to Babe's 714 total. Al Simmons, Mack's left fielder, pulled his left foot back away from the plate when he was at bat, like a timid kid fearful of the pitcher. He was the only player who could ever hit with that one-foot-in-the-bucket style, as players say. He had an eleven-year stretch in which he was only twice under .340. Twice he led the league with marks of .381 and .390. Mickey Cochrane could hit, too. He averaged .346 for the three years of the Athletics' championship teams and he was a fiery and inspiring competitor. As for Lefty Grove, he is in the select circle of pitchers who have won 300 or more games. There are only seven since the turn of the century.

The A's looked something like the 1927 Yankees in the pennant race of 1929. They made a cakewalk of it, tallying 104 victories and leading the deflated Yankees by eighteen games.

In the National League, the Chicago Cubs, powered by Hornsby's .380 average and Hack Wilson's 159 runs batted in, took the flag with ten and a half games to spare. They were managed by Joe McCarthy, a relative newcomer who had never worn a major-league uniform as a player.

The capacity crowd of 50,740 spectators at the Cubs' Wrigley Field on October 8 at the 1929 Series opener thought that senility had at last caught up with Connie Mack when 35-year-old Howard Ehmke was announced as his starting pitcher. Ehmke had not pitched in six weeks and was 'way past his prime. During the regular season he had gone the distance only twice. Fans could not understand why the choice wasn't Lefty Grove, or George Earnshaw, or Rube Walberg, all of whom were regulars and consistent winners.

Why Ehmke? It was a secret between the oldtimer and Connie. A few weeks before the Series, Connie had gently told Ehmke that he would have to let him go.

"I'm not surprised," replied Ehmke. "I haven't been much help but I've always wanted to pitch in a World Series game and I'm sure I've got one more good game left in me."

Surprisingly, Connie agreed with Ehmke and told the pitcher to quietly scout the Cubs while the A's were on the road. "See what they like and don't like to hit," he said, "and I'll pitch you in the first game. But don't tell a soul."

Shrewd old Connie had a hunch that Ehmke's slow, breaking stuff would baffle the Cubs, who would be expecting to face the fireballing of Grove or Earnshaw. It might throw them completely off stride, he reasoned.

Never did such a hunch pay off so well. Ehmke had the Cubs at his mercy. He struck out thirteen, a Series record, and did not yield a run until the ninth inning. He won, 3 to 1, but that was his last gasp. He never won another game. Connie always called that game his supreme thrill.

He might have picked the fourth game for thrills, for it still stands as one of the most exciting, slam-bang affairs in Series history. It took place in Philadelphia on October 12. The Cubs had won their first game the day before and the Series now stood two games to one in the A's favor.

It looked like another win for the Cubs when they scored two runs in the fourth, five more in the sixth, and picked up another one in the seventh. When the A's came to bat in their half of the seventh they were behind, 8 to 0, and had made only three hits all afternoon.

Al Simmons opened the seventh with a homer to polite but re-strained applause. At least, it wasn't going to be a shutout. Connie was about to remove his regulars to give some substitutes a chance to play in a World Series, but Foxx followed Simmons with a single and then in rapid succession came three more singles and the A's now had three runs.

George Burns batted for the A's pitcher, Ed Rommel, and popped out, but second baseman Max Bishop smacked another single to score Jimmy Dykes for a fourth run. At this point the fans began to sit up and take notice. They were soon turned into wild-eyed maniacs.

To the plate came center fielder Mule Haas and sent a well-hit fly ball to center. It was apparently a routine out, but Hack Wilson, who came after the ball, suddenly was blinded by the sun and lost it completely. The ball skidded into deepest center while Haas, running like a greyhound, beat the relay to the plate. Two runners scored ahead of him and now the A's were trailing by only one run, 8 to 7.

There was more to come as manager McCarthy frantically shut-tled pitchers back and forth. Cochrane walked, Simmons and Foxx singled, and Cochrane scored the tying run. Right fielder Bing Miller got hit by a pitched ball, filling the bases, and when Jimmy Dykes a moment later rammed a double to left, two more runs came in — the ninth and tenth — in this most explosive inning in Series history. At

One of baseball's most effective batteries when the Philadelphia Athletics were tops in the American League for the last time (1929–1931) consisted of Mickey Cochrane (above) and Lefty Grove (right).

last the Cubs retired the side as the next two batters struck out. Oddly, two of the three outs were contributed by Mack's pinch hitters.

The end came in the next game, which was also a thriller but was an anticlimax after the unprecedented come-from-behind slaughter that had preceded it. The A's were behind, 2–0, in the ninth inning of the fifth game, when they staged a three-run rally to win, 3 to 2. That was the Series. A grateful Philadelphia presented Connie Mack with the Bok Award as the citizen who had done the greatest service for the city in 1929, an annual honor that never before or since has been bestowed upon a baseball figure.

The A's continued to dominate the league in 1930, with "Bucketfoot Al" Simmons hitting .381 for top honors, two points better than the mark of runner-up Lou Gehrig. They won the flag almost as easily

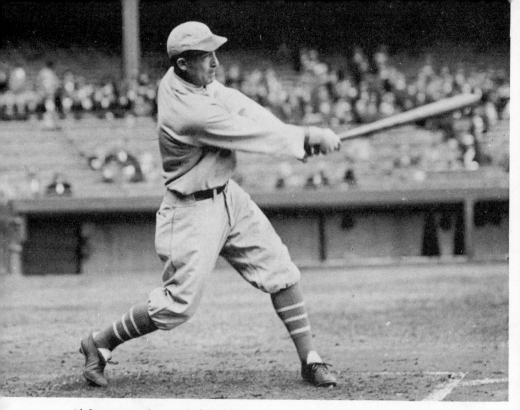

Al Simmons, the A's left fielder, had an unusual foot-in-the-bucket batting stance, but he was an outstanding hitter. In one ten-year stretch he hit .340 or higher nine times.

as the year before but met sterner World Series opposition in the St. Louis Cardinals, a colorful, hustling aggregation that was just becoming known as the "Gas House Gang."

The A's subdued them in six games, however, behind the great pitching of Grove and Earnshaw, each of whom won two games. That was all the A's needed for their second consecutive World Championship.

Could they make it three in a row, a feat that no team had yet accomplished? Connie Mack had often said, "A champion is not great unless he repeats." Now he said, "A champion must win three times in succession to be truly great."

Connie's inspired boys bludgeoned their way through the league in 1931 and chalked up 107 victories against forty-five defeats to win easily, thirteen and a half games in front of the Yankees. Al Simmons hit .390 for his second consecutive league batting title and Lefty Grove had a magnificent 31–4 season. The other two pitchers of Connie's

"Big Three," Earnshaw and Walberg, were in the twenty-game winning circle. The "Big Three" accounted for seventy-two of the team's 107 wins. In contrast, the National League did not produce a single twenty-game winner.

This was a repeat Series. The Cardinals had a sound, well-balanced club with Frankie Frisch on second, Chick Hafey, the National League batting champion (.349), in left field, and Jim Bottomley (.348) on first.

They also had a squat, barrel-chested center fielder named John Leonard (Pepper) Martin who, at 27, had completed his first full major-league season that year with an even .300 batting average, but he had provided the spark that had helped the Cards to their second straight flag. He was a reckless and fierce competitor, and he looked it. He had the craggy features of a pirate cutthroat; he was usually unshaven and his uniform was nearly always torn and dirty because of his famous head-first slides.

The A's were heavily favored to take the Series as the teams met in the first game at Sportsman's Park, St. Louis, on October 1, 1931, with the unbeatable Grove on the mound. As expected, the Athletics won but not before Martin let them know that it was going to be his party. On his first trip to the plate he slashed a double off the right field wall, followed it up with two singles, and made a belly-slide steal of second.

This was the start of one of the most spectacular one-man shows ever seen in the World Series. After the first game, Martin sought out his manager, Gabby Street, and pleaded, "Let me run on that Mickey Cochrane, Gabby." And run he did the next day in such a manner that he had the A's dizzy and the fans howling with excitement.

In the second inning he stretched a single into a double, arriving head-first at second, then a moment later he broke for third and beat Cochrane's rifle throw in a swirl of dust. On a fly to center he came home with the first Cardinal run. In the seventh he was off again like a wild man. He singled, stole second, took third on an infield out, and hurled himself across the plate as Earnshaw, fielding a squeeze bunt, threw frantically to Cochrane. Martin's runs were the only two of the game.

No longer was the grim little scrapper a comparatively unknown rookie. When the Cards came to Philadelphia on October 5 for the third game, Pepper's name led all the rest. The Philadelphia fans were with him almost to a man, cheering him roundly as he responded with a single and a double and made two runs for a 5–2 Cardinal victory.

It was Martin again the next day. Big George Earnshaw allowed only two hits, both of which came from the bat of the amazing Pepper — a single and a double. For good measure he stole another base. Humorist H. I. Phillips, writing in the *New York Sun,* summed up the fourth game, as follows: "The World Series being played this year between the Philadelphia Athletics and Pepper Martin of Temple, Oklahoma, resulted in a victory for the Athletics, 3 to 0."

The grimy-uniformed Martin had captured the fancy of the nation by this time. Hitting, stealing, bluffing steals, snagging flies on the run, he electrified the fans and gave the A's a fine case of jitters. In the fifth game, although nipped by Cochrane for the first time on an attempted steal, he had another great day. He beat out a bunt in the fourth inning, smashed a homer in the sixth, and singled in the eighth. He batted in four of the Cards' five runs and the 5–1 victory gave them a three-to-two edge in games. At this point the amazing Martin had made twelve hits in eighteen times at bat for a .667 average, far beyond the Babe's .625 record Series average.

The wild man could not hold it, however. Back in St. Louis his hitting streak came to an end, although he did not go into total eclipse. He went hitless in the sixth game, which the A's won, 8 to 1. The Series was now tied at three games each.

In the deciding game, Pepper drew a walk in the first inning and promptly stole second (his fifth steal of the Series). He failed again to hit and wound up with a .500 average, but it was still his party. In the ninth when the A's were trailing by two runs, they put the tying runs on base with two out. Max Bishop then hit a low liner that looked like a certain hit, but Pepper dashed in from center to make a one-handed stab for the final out, thus ending the Series and giving the Cards the World Championship.

In the clubhouse after the game, Commissioner Judge Landis congratulated the grinning Pepper and said, "Young man, if I could change places with anyone in the world today, it would be you."

"It's all right with me, Judge," said the Series hero, "just as long as we change salaries, too. My $4,500 a year for your $65,000."

The A's were still a fine team in 1932, but they had had their run and perhaps they were surfeited with victory, or perhaps the

Yankees had the better ball team. At any rate, they ran second to the Yankees, who were now managed by Joe McCarthy, the former pilot of the Chicago Cubs. William Wrigley, owner of the Cubs, had let McCarthy go because he wanted "somebody who can get me a World Championship."

The Cubs won the National League pennant in 1932 and McCarthy at last had a chance to even the score with his former employers. Joe's revenge was sweet. The Yankees crushed the Cubs in four straight.

The Series would be recorded as just another one-sided Yankee sweep except for a famous Ruthian episode in the third game at Chicago. With the score tied 4–4 in the fifth inning, the Babe, who had homered in the first, came to bat. The crowd had heckled him all during the game and now the fans whooped it up more than ever.

Charlie Root, the Cubs' pitcher, put one across the plate and Ruth took the strike and then defiantly pointed deep into the center field bleachers. He took another strike and repeated the gesture, showing in pantomine just where he intended to hit the ball. The crowd booed and hooted. Root did not waste a pitch and sent the third one right down the middle. Sure enough, the Big Fellow connected solidly and the ball sailed to the deepest point in the center field bleachers, a really terrific wallop. Ruth, the perfect showman, trotted around the bases shaking with laughter as he received his greatest ovation.

Charlie Root has since said that it never happened, that Ruth was merely holding up his fingers to denote the number of strikes. Some sportswriters, who were not there, have tried to debunk the story. However, almost all the 400 baseball scribes who saw the game agree that Ruth did call the shot. Umpire George Magerkurth who was behind the plate always said that Ruth called it. Ruth himself said so and Lou Gehrig also did. They should know. In any event, it was without doubt the most magnificent gesture ever made on a baseball diamond, one that could only come from the game's most colorful and dynamic figure.

After the 1932 slaughter of the Cubs the Yankees skidded into a short-lived decline. The Babe began to slip rapidly (.301 in 1933) and it was apparent that he was on his way out.

Across the river from the Bronx Bombers, the Giants came to life again under the management of first baseman Bill Terry, the National

League's last .400 hitter (he hit .401 in 1930). Terry had been picked by the ailing McGraw to be his successor, and although he was never popular among the sportswriting fraternity because of his brusque manner, he was a good leader and a managerial success from the start. He played a whale of a first base, too, averaging .340 during his five-year reign as playing manager (1932–1936). Terry lifted the Giants from sixth place in 1932 to first in one year and went on to win two more pennants in his brief career.

His first flag winner carried only two explosive bats, his own and Mel Ott's, and invited comparison with the White Sox Hitless Wonders of 1906. Little Mel Ott, out in right field, was a home run hitter and an excellent ball hawk. He wore the Giant uniform for twenty-two years and never any other one.

Carl Hubbell, one of the game's great left-handers, was Terry's pitching ace. Known as "King Carl" and also as the "Meal Ticket" because of his reliability, Hubbell was a screwball artist without peer.

The 1933 club also had spirit, as exemplified by Blondy Ryan, the rookie shortstop, in his famous telegram. He had recovered from an injury and was about to rejoin the team, which was then in a slump. "They can't beat us. En route, J. G. Ryan," wired the inspired freshman who was only a .238 hitter. Nevertheless, the slump ended with Blondy's return to the lineup.

The Washington Senators, managed by 26-year-old Joe Cronin who played shortstop, led the Yankees by seven games in the American League race and faced the Giants in the 1933 World Series. There was not much to it. The New Yorkers won easily, 4–1, as Carl Hubbell won two games and Mel Ott hit two homers and batted .389. John McGraw lived just long enough to see the galling defeat of 1924 avenged. He died the following February.

A fighting, rip-snorting, colorful ball club known as the Gas House Gang came to the fore in the National League in 1934 and brought home another pennant to St. Louis. The Cardinals that year won the admiration of baseball addicts with their aggressiveness, the win-at-any-cost game they played. They were blood relatives to the old Orioles and to the early Giants of McGraw. It was the first ball club in years that had a definite personality and it became one of the best box-office attractions in National League history.

Stars of the championship Cardinals in the nineteen-thirties were: Pepper Martin (left), who ran wild against the A's in 1931, and Dizzy Dean (right) who hurled two victories against the Tigers in 1934.

Pepper Martin, the Wild Horse of the Osage, as he was now called, was at third base and was as spectacular there as he had been at chasing flies. Never a graceful player, he would block the hottest grounders with his chest and get his man with a rifle throw.

Ducky Medwick, a powerful hitter and a willing scrapper (he fought with his teammates as well as with the enemy) was in left field. A dangerous bad-ball hitter, he could wallop almost anything. There was no way to pitch to him.

Leo Durocher, at his playing and talking peak, was the shortstop; Rip Collins, a graceful switch-hitter was on first, and Frankie Frisch, the playing manager, was on second.

Jay Hanna Dean, known as Dizzy, and his brother Paul, known as Daffy, were the mainstays of the pitching staff. Daffy joined the club in 1934 and when he arrived, Dizzy, who had been with the Cards for four years, said, "That kid brother of mine is a better pitcher'n me. Me'n' Paul will win fifty games this year."

They almost did. Dizzy, who might have been one of the all-time greats if an injury had not cut short his career, won thirty games (he lost only seven) and Brother Paul won nineteen, with eleven losses. That totaled just one short of Dizzy's boasted fifty.

When the Cards won the pennant and were preparing to face the Detroit Tigers in the World Series, Dizzy said to reporters: "Who won the pennant? Me 'n' Paul. Who's goin' to win the Series? Me 'n' Paul."

Never a shrinking violet, Dizzy used to stop strangers on the street and ask them were the ball park was. Then he would introduce himself as, "The Great Dean, the most fastest pitcher since David hurled the slingshot." His brag was not far off. He had tremendous speed and a variety of hooks and slants.

Mickey Cochrane in his first year as manager of the Tigers caught 129 games, batted, .320, and was the prime factor in bringing them home first. It was a solid club with a pair of outstanding performers in second baseman Charley Gehringer and Hank Greenberg at first. Reliable but unspectacular Charley Gehringer, who was called the Mechanical Man, was consistently in the .300 circle in his eighteen consecutive seasons with the Tigers and one year (1937) he won the league batting crown with .371. Hank Greenberg was also a .300 hitter for years and had great power at the plate. He smashed out fifty-eight homers for the Tigers in 1938. Both Gehringer and Greenberg are in baseball's Hall of Fame.

Dizzy Dean made good his boast about "Me 'n' Paul" winning the 1934 Series. Each won two games, just as he had said they would, but they had plenty of trouble doing it. Dizzy won the first game but the Tigers took the second. Brother Paul won the third for the Cards and then, following the same pattern, the Tigers won the next one. In that game Dizzy was sent in as a pinch runner in the fourth inning and was promptly hit in the head by a thrown ball as he ran for second. He went out cold and was carried off the field to a hospital, where it was announced that he was through for the Series.

However, the next day there was the Dizzy one on the mound (with a goose egg on his forehead), but he was not quite up to standard. The Tigers' Tommy Bridges beat him, 3 to 1. Brother Paul squared the Series the following day by winning, 4 to 3, and in the final game at Detroit it was Dizzy's turn again.

It was a contest until the third inning, when the Cards exploded with a seven-run broadside. Dizzy himself contributed to the onslaught with his bat, making two hits before the inning was over, thus becoming (as his plaque in the Hall of Fame records) "first pitcher to make two hits in one inning in World Series."

In the sixth inning, with the Cards ahead by 9–0, Medwick belted a triple and slid hard into Marvin Owen, covering third. For a moment the two men tangled.

Later, when Medwick ran out to his position in left field, he was greeted with a bombardment of rolled-up newspapers, garbage, and bottles from the angry bleacherites. He walked away while the groundkeepers removed the refuse, but as soon as he returned a new shower fell upon him. The game was held up for twenty minutes.

Judge Landis summoned the umpires to his box and held a conference. "Get your man out of the game," he told manager Frankie Frisch.

"But why should I take him out?" asked Frisch. "He hasn't done anything. Suppose it costs me the game?"

The Judge glanced at the scoreboard, which said St. Louis 9, Detroit 0. "If you can lose this one, your team needs a new manager," he said coldly. "Get him out of there, I want to see the game finished."

With Chick Fullis in left field, the Cards scored two more runs to win, 11 to 0.

The Tigers had a happier time of it the following year when they again won the flag and met the Chicago Cubs in the World Series. It was the same club that had lost to the Cards, but this time the Tigers conquered their Series jinx and defeated the Cubs in six games. Thus, in 1935 after four unsuccessful tries for a World Championship (going back to 1907), the Tigers finally won one.

Joe McCarthy and Babe Ruth barely spoke to each other while Joe managed
the Yankees. The pilot brought eight pennants and seven World Championships to New York during his reign (1931 to May, 1946).

CHAPTER **7**

FOUR STRAIGHT

(1936–1939)

THE YEAR of the Gas House Gang, when the Tigers took their beatings as rubbish fell from the skies, was a bad one for the greatest Yankee of them all. In 1934 Babe Ruth dropped below .300 for the first time since the disastrous year of 1925 and it was obvious to everyone that he was nearing the end of the trail. He was 39, beefier than ever around the middle (he weighed around 280) and had slowed down. He hit .288 that season and made only twenty-two home runs.

Perhaps the Babe began to lose some of his zest for the game as far back as 1929, when manager Miller Huggins died suddenly and Bob Shawkey got the job. Shawkey was a likable veteran who had become a Yankee coach after he retired as a pitcher. The Babe knew that his playing days were nearly over and he wanted to become manager of the Yankees more than he had ever wanted anything else. He was greatly disappointed when Bob Shawkey was picked. Ed Barrow, the club's business manager, has said that Ruth was never for a moment even considered for the job. "After all," said Barrow, who was well aware of the Babe's rollicking behavior off the field and his reluctance to go to bed, "Ruth couldn't manage himself."

The arrival of Joe McCarthy in 1931 as the Yankees' new manager (Shawkey was fired) caused a rift in the club. Some of the players thought that Ruth should have been given the job and they resented the presence of McCarthy. Others agreed with Barrow that Ruth would never make a good manager.

It was not easy for McCarthy to take the helm when he did, knowing that Ruth, the super-star, would be aligned against him. Consider what McCarthy, who had never been a big-league ball player, had to face: Ruth was then making $80,000 a year, more than twice the amount McCarthy earned as the head man and supposedly Ruth's boss. More than that, the Babe was living like a prima donna. He occupied a hotel suite on the road instead of a double room with a teammate; he had his own drawing room on trains; he kept his own hours and was a law unto himself. His wife traveled with him most of the time.

From the beginning Ruth and McCarthy never hit it off and neither went to any great pains to conceal their dislike of each other. McCarthy never gave Ruth any direct orders. Had the Babe been just a fine player who was slowing up fast, McCarthy would have benched him. But he was Ruth, the one and only, who had become a baseball tradition in his own time, and McCarthy watched him in silence and let him take himself out of the lineup or put himself in whenever he wanted to. Few words passed between the two, but the Babe was often critical of McCarthy in the hearing of other players and newspapermen.

At the end of the 1934 season, during which the Babe had taken himself out of perhaps fifty games, Ruth told Jake Ruppert that he was dissatisfied with McCarthy and wanted to manage the Yankees himself. Ruppert thought for a moment and then asked Ruth if he would like to manage Newark, an International League club owned by the Yankee organization. If he proved himself there as a manager, he might eventually take over the Yankees, suggested Ruppert.

"No," said Ruth angrily. "I won't go to Newark or any other minor-league club. I'm a big leaguer and I'm going to stay one." He stormed out of the Yankee owner's office.

Ruppert knew then that the Babe's usefulness to the Yankees had ended. He had offered him a way out but Ruth had flatly turned it down. In February, 1935, Ruth was given his unconditional release and went to the Boston Braves, where he had an unhappy time and departed after appearing in only twenty-eight games. Before leaving, he hit his last homer, number 714, on May 25 in Pittsburgh. It was one of a cluster of three hit in the game.

The loss of the Babe came as the Yankees were on the threshold of a drive that would sweep them into power for another long period. It is significant that with the Babe's departure, Joe McCarthy began to move. He was helped, of course — if "helped" isn't too mild a word to use here — by the entrance upon the Yankee stage of Joseph Paul DiMaggio, Jr., a young San Franciscan who had been burning up the Pacific Coast League with his sensational hitting. In 1935 the 21-year-old Italian-American outfielder hit .398 and clouted thirty-four homers for the San Francisco Seals. Major League scouts had been hot on his trail since his freshman year in 1933 with the Seals as a regular outfielder, when he hit safely in sixty-one consecutive games, a league record. An off-the-field accident to his knee cooled most of the scouts off, however. The rumor got around that Joe suffered from "chronic knee trouble." The Yankee scouts checked into the rumors and decided to take a chance on him. They got DiMag for $25,000. It proved to be the greatest bargain in the history of modern baseball.

Included in the scouts' report was the comment that "DiMaggio is more than just a great hitter. Everybody talks about his hitting, but he is the best center fielder since Tris Speaker."

Once in Yankee uniform (in 1936), Joe convinced McCarthy, his teammates, and the baseball writers that the stories of his skill and power were not exaggerated. He had never seen major-league pitching before, but he hit it with ease and he patrolled left field, which was the difficult sunfield at Yankee Stadium, as if he had been born there. (He was later shifted to center field because he could cover such a wide range of territory.)

The apparently indestructible Lou Gehrig, who hadn't missed a game in over ten years, was still on first. He who had walked so long in the Babe's shadow, now walked in the shadow of the rookie DiMaggio. He did not mind, though, as he was a team player first of all and Joe did not swagger in his new role.

Tony Lazzeri and Frank Crosetti, the veteran second-base combination, sparked the infield. Red Rolfe of Dartmouth was on third and was fast becoming the league's best player at that position. Jake Powell and George Selkirk, two .300 hitters, were in the outfield with Joe. Catcher Bill Dickey was at his peak and there was no better backstop in the game. A strong pitching staff included Red Ruffing, Lefty Gomez, Monte Pearson, Bump Hadley, and Pat Malone.

As the club rolled through June and piled up a comfortable lead, there was no doubt about who was going to win the pennant in the American League. The team had everything. Sportswriters began calling them the new Murderers' Row.

By August the other clubs in the league had folded and on September 9 the Yankees clinched the flag, then went on to finish nineteen and a half games in front of the Tigers.

Not since 1927 had baseball seen such power at the plate as was displayed by the 1936 Bronx Bombers. Five Yankees batted in 100 or more runs: Gehrig (152), DiMaggio (125), Lazzeri (109), Dickey (107), and Selkirk (107). With the exception of Crosetti and Lazzeri, all the regulars batted better than .300.

For the first time since 1923, baseball had a "Subway Series," as the Giants had taken the National League flag after a hard battle against the contending Cardinals and Cubs. What made the Giant victory possible was Carl Hubbell's invincible pitching. The "Meal Ticket" was consistently superb. He won sixteen games in a row and was stopped only because the 1936 season ended and the schedule ran out of games for him to pitch. He carried the streak into the next season, to notch twenty-four all told without a defeat. This is baseball's longest winning streak for a pitcher, but because it was divided into two seasons, it is denied recognition in the record book.

What little pleasure the Giants got out of their fourth World Series with their rivals from across the Harlem River came from the steady left arm of Carl Hubbell, who won the first game, 6 to 1.

The memory of the second game still makes Giant fans wince. The Bombers turned on the fireworks in this one, as President Franklin D. Roosevelt applauded in his box near the Giants' dugout. They shelled four Giant pitchers for eighteen runs, the most ever made by a team in a World Series. Every player on the Yankees made a hit and scored a run. Dickey and Lazzeri hit homers, Tony's coming with the bases loaded in the third inning. Not since 1920 when Cleveland's Elmer Smith hit a jackpot home run against the Dodgers, had this feat been accomplished in a Series. Tony at last had made amends for his humiliating strikeout by Old Pete Alexander in the 1926 Series, when three Yankees died on base. The final score after nearly three hours of play was 18 to 4.

Another kind of agony was in store for Giant fans in the third game. The teams went to the eighth inning with the score tied at 1–1

Boyish-looking Joe DiMaggio is congratulated by Commissioner Judge Landis for being the outstanding rookie of 1936. The onlookers are New York's mayor, F. H. LaGuardia (far left), and Col. Jacob Ruppert, owner of the Yankees.

with Fred Fitzsimmons on the mound for the Giants. Fitz had pitched great ball from the start and had held the Yankees to two hits, one of which was a homer by Gehrig. The Giants, meanwhile, had made eleven hits but they had been able to put only one run across, a homer by outfielder Jimmy Ripple.

In the fatal eighth, Selkirk opened with a single, Powell walked, and Lazzeri moved them along with a sacrifice. Red Ruffing slapped weakly to Fitzsimmons, who nailed Selkirk at the plate. Crosetti came to bat and hit a high bounder just to the right of the box. Fitzsimmons, who was the best fielding pitcher in baseball, went after it but the ball glanced off his glove and Powell came home with what proved to be the winning run. His eyes streaming with tears of rage, Fitz retired the side but the Giants did nothing for him when they came to bat and the Yankees chalked up a 2–1 victory. Even Joe McCarthy felt sorry for Fitz that day.

After that there wasn't much to it, although the Giants won one more ,a ten-inning 5–4 decision. In the final game the Giants again felt the power of the Yankees' bats in a seventeen-hit assault which gave the Bombers a 13–5 victory and the Series at four games to two.

The 1937 season was almost the same as the preceding one for the Yankees. Again they won the pennant in early September with 102 games and again there was no other club in the league within sight of them. They dominated everything that year, including the All-Star Game which was played in Washington on July 7.

Joe McCarthy, as manager of the American League All-Star team, picked five Yankees in his starting lineup for the game: Rolfe, DiMaggio, Gehrig, Dickey, and Gomez. As expected, they stole the show and won it for the league, 8 to 3.

At the season's end the Yankees were again the unanimous choice to repeat in another Subway Series — and they did it with ease. The Giants furnished even less opposition than they had the year before, winning only one game this time. It was Carl Hubbell who supplied the lone Giant victory. In the fourth game he managed to harness the Yankees with a 7–3 decision. In the two Subway Series the Giants had taken only three games, two of which were won by faithful Carl.

After the Series, in which, incidentally, Lazzeri led his team with an average of .400, Tony was released by the Yankees and went to the Chicago Cubs with the hope of eventually managing the club. This left behind only one survivor of the original Murderers' Row of 1927 — Lou Gehrig. Now, ten years later, the new Murderers' Row was being compared favorably to the old one by many baseball experts.

To be sure, the 1937 Yankees had nothing near the color of the boisterous crew managed by Miller Huggins in Ruth's heyday, nor did they have its awesome power at the plate. But they won just as easily, like the well-oiled, efficient machine they were. In fact, they so far excelled the other seven clubs in the American League that the top-heavy situation was described by sportswriters outside of New York as "Snow White and the Seven Dwarfs." The American League was indeed a one-team circuit.

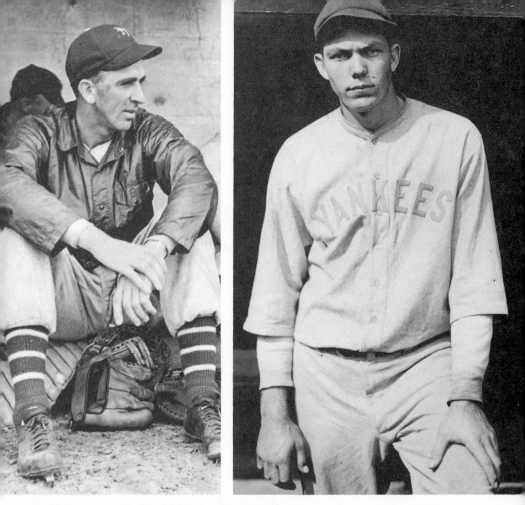

(Left) Southpaw Carl Hubbell, the Giants' brilliant moundsman of the 1930–1940 era, pitched twenty-four consecutive victories (sixteen in 1936 and eight in 1937) before he was stopped. (Right) One of the reasons for the continued success of the Yankees was their superb catcher, Bill Dickey, whose playing career lasted from 1928 to 1946.

The absolute supremacy of the Bronx Bombers was no accident, of course. The Yankee organization with millions in the till was a no-nonsense business operation. It was run efficiently and staffed by the best brains in baseball. It had the best business manager in Ed Barrow. It had the best scouts and the most successful farm teams, such as Newark, Binghamton, Kansas City, Norfolk, and Akron, which were consistent pennant winners in their various leagues.

The other American League clubs criticized the Yankees for destroying all semblance of balance in their own league and making the World Series no more than a one-team exhibition. One manager bitterly commented at the beginning of the 1938 season, "If the Yankees don't win the pennant by August first, there ought to be a Grand Jury investigation."

Such talk always irritated the bachelor owner of the Yankees, multi-millionaire Jake Ruppert. "They say that we have a monopoly on all good young ball players, that we run away with the pennants," he said in an interview with a baseball writer. "Well, do they think I should help the weaker clubs by giving them Yankee stars and the pick of players on my minor league farms? Nonsense," snorted Ruppert. "Why find fault with the Yankees because they represent the best? Why not find fault with the other clubs for not being better? They should not worry about the Yankees. They should worry about themselves."

Pounding the table in his brewery, Ruppert continued, "I spent years and money building an efficient organization. I have a five million dollar investment in it, and now that it's working smoothly, should I give it away? No. I want to win. Every day I want to win, ten to nothing. Close games make me nervous."

The machine-like Joe McCarthy, who had the personality of a stone, rarely gave Ruppert much to get nervous about as the Yankees continued along the victory path winning by decisive scores.

It was not roses all the way, however. The Yankees got off to an uncertain start in the spring of 1938 when Joe DiMaggio remained in San Francisco because his demand for a $40,000 salary had been turned down by the club. Ruppert revealed that he had offered Joe $25,000, which was an increase over the previous season and more than DiMag had ever been paid in his life. After all, the owner reasoned, in the midst of a big depression, $40,000 was a pretty stiff asking price for a young player with only two years of major-league ball behind him.

Joe's teammates thought so, too. They did not like it when he failed to show up at St. Petersburg to get in shape with them for the coming campaign. His playing might make the difference between another flag and second-place money. Stubbornly, Joe held out and was not on hand for the early games. (This was the third consecutive season that Joe had failed to be in the lineup at the start, but his absence had been caused by injuries in his rookie and sophomore years.)

Meanwhile the Yankees got under way with a new second baseman to replace Tony Lazzeri. He was Joe (Flash) Gordon, an acrobatic youngster up from Newark. It was plain from the day he played his first major-league game that he was going to be a standout, a Yankee fixture for years to come — and he was. Another addition was Babe Dahlgren, a first baseman if Iron Horse Gehrig should ever need a replacement. That possibility seemed as far off as ever, with Lou still playing every game, still hitting like a demon (.354 in 1936, .351 in 1937).

DiMag finally yielded and reported two weeks late, but did not start until April 30. While his teammates forgave him, he experienced something new the first time he went to bat at the Stadium. The fans booed him, and they kept booing him all around the circuit. The impassive, uncomplaining DiMaggio took it in stride but he felt it, nevertheless.

From July on, the 1938 pennant race was another Yankee breeze. The flag was clinched on September 18, and in the final reckoning the team finished nine and a half games ahead of the Red Sox.

In the National League the Cubs barely nosed out the Pirates in a late September finish to lead them by two games. The pennant was settled in dramatic fashion by a home run hit by the Cubs' catcher-manager, Gabby Hartnett, in the last half of the ninth inning in semi-darkness in a "winner-take-all" game with the Pirates. Almost every baseball fan in the country, with the exception of the Yankee faithful, was hoping for a Chicago victory in the Series after such a heroic finish — but no, it was not to be.

McCarthy's wreckers could not be stopped and they won in the shortest time possible, which is to say, in four straight games. Big crowds turned out to see the first two contests in Chicago, but in New York at the third and fourth games there were huge gaps of empty seats in the Stadium. At any rate, McCarthy had accomplished something that no other manager had ever done before. He had won three consecutive World Championships. As for the unfortunate Cubs, it was their sixth straight Series reverse since 1910.

Baseball fans in the fall of 1938 were buzzing more about what had happened to Lou Gehrig than they were about the one-sided

Joe (Flash) Gordon replaced Tony Lazzeri at second base for the Yankees and immediately became a star.

Series. The Iron Horse, as usual, had gone through the season without missing a game, but he had failed to hit .300 or better for the first time in thirteen years. His batting average of .295 and his twenty-nine home runs because of a good start would satisfy almost anyone except Lou. It was far off the pace for him. It was the Series which finally showed that something had happened to Lou. He was slow and he hit only four singles in the four games and did not drive in a run.

The club cut Lou's salary by $4,000 the following winter, but he made no complaint. At $35,000 a year he was still one of the highest paid ball players in the game. All of his thoughts that winter were on staging a comeback. He put in countless hours of exercising in the gym and working outdoors.

For all his work, Lou was far below form at the Yankees' training quarters at St. Petersburg in the spring of 1939. Ground balls were going past him as though first base were vacant. He was clumsy and awkward and he had no power at the plate. He could not hit the ball out of the infield.

Lou was nearly 36, an age at which many athletes slow down, but his trouble went deeper than that. It went beyond the mere fading of youth. He was afflicted with a form of chronic infantile paralysis, although no one knew it at the time, including Lou. One of the symptoms of this always fatal disease is a gradual loss of coordination and strength.

With the opening of the season, Lou looked worse than ever before. He played eight games, and then on the morning of May 2, 1939, when the Yankees were in Detroit, he sorrowfully said to McCarthy, "I'm benching myself, Joe. Put Babe Dahlgren on first today."

"Why?" asked the manager, although he already knew the answer.

"I'm not doing the club any good out there. I just can't seem to get going," Lou replied.

That afternoon for the first time since June 1, 1925, Gehrig sat in the dugout as the Yankees took the field. His string of 2,130 consecutive games had at last been broken.

With Lou on the bench (he was made non-playing captain), Babe Dahlgren, a .235 hitter, stepped in and played a good defensive game, but things were not the same around first. The outfield was greatly strengthened by the addition of Charley (King Kong) Keller, a swarthy, broad-shouldered Marylander who had come from the Yankees' Newark farm. With Tommy Henrich, another Newark alumnus, in right field and the great DiMag in center, the Yankees had one of the best outfields seen in years.

Could the Yankees do it again without Gehrig? was the question that was making the rounds in baseball circles. The answer was not long in coming, and it was yes, they could. In typical relentless, monotonous Yankee fashion, the club bulled through the league in 1939 and took the pennant by a margin of seventeen games over the Red Sox, winning a total of 106 games against forty-five defeats.

The team that opposed the Yankee juggernaut that fall was the surprising Cincinnati Reds. It was the first pennant the city had seen since the dark days of 1919. The Yankees were, of course, favored to take the Series, although there was some talk about the Reds being a "team of destiny."

Then came the Series and the Reds were suffocated in four consecutive games. In all fairness, however, they went down gamely and with a couple of breaks they might have won two games. In the first game, for example, with the scored tied at 1–1 in the ninth inning, Keller hit a fly to right center that might have been caught by Ival Goodman, but it slipped off his finger tips and Keller made third. A few moments later he trotted in with the winning run as Bill Dickey punched out a single.

The Reds should have won the final game in Cincinnati, which they handed to the Yankees. Up until then they had played errorless ball throughout the Series, but they began to stagger in the ninth inning, when they had a two-run lead and a perfect double-play ball was botched by shortstop Billy Myers. The miscue gave the Yankees two unearned runs for a 4–4 tie and kept the game alive.

It was worse for the Reds in the tenth. Frank Crosetti, the first man up, walked and Rolfe sacrificed him to second. Keller hit a routine grounder to Billy Myers, who, brooding no doubt over his frightful error of the previous inning, muffed this one, too. Crosetti went to third. Then DiMag came to bat and poked out a single to right. It turned out to be just as good as a home run. Goodman, in right field, fumbled the ball as Crosetti scored, then retrieved it and made a long throw to the plate to cut down Keller, who was roaring home like a tank. The throw came to big Ernie Lombardi, the Reds' 270-pound catcher. Just as Lombardi grabbed the throw, Keller churned into him and sent him sprawling. Big Ernie lay stunned, the ball no more than two feet from him. DiMaggio, seeing the giant catcher flat and motionless, kept right on running and crossed the plate before the hapless Lombardi could gather his wits. The three Yankee runs gave them a 7–4 victory.

The incident has since become famous as "Lombardi's snooze at the plate," but the catcher has not deserved the ridicule that has been heaped upon him. He was, after all, badly shaken up and stunned, as who wouldn't be after a collision with the burley, hard-running Keller? Ernie was twice the National League batting champion and was once voted its most valuable player, but the "snooze" episode still clings to him.

McCarthy had now not only tied Connie Mack with five World Championships, but he had won four in a row, the last two of which were "clean sweeps." Such a record called for a celebration, or so some of the Yankee players thought as their special train rolled toward New York after the final game in Cincinnati.

They paraded through the car and came to McCarthy's drawing room. Someone knocked on the door. McCarthy opened it, stuck his head out and barked sharply, "Cut that college stuff out! This is a major-league club!" The door slammed shut.

CHAPTER **8**

THE DOLDRUMS

(1940–1946)

THE 1940 SEASON was played under the shadow of the war that was raging throughout Europe. The forces of Hitler and Mussolini had swept the continent in triumphant marches. France, beaten to her knees that summer, surrendered to Germany, and England reeled under Hitler's large-scale air attacks. The Battle of Britain was on.

In this country, 16,000,000 men between the ages of 21 and 36 registered for a year of training and service in the armed forces. It was our first peacetime military draft and the shift of manpower was felt everywhere. Soon, we were in the fight with the rest of the world. Baseball entered the doldrums after Pearl Harbor, when almost every player of consequence was in uniform. Talent reached an all-time low in the majors. Draft-exempt players who could not have made a minor-league team in peacetime found themselves in big-league uniforms, as exemplified by the one-armed outfielder, Pete Gray, who played seventy-seven games for the St. Louis Browns in 1945. (see photo)

The 1940 season was a fairly normal one, however, except for one thing. It was the year the Yankees did not win the pennant. They slipped to third place and it was just as well for baseball that they did. Fans were getting tired of them. The club was the same but some of the players were beginning to show their age. Even so, they finished only two games behind the pennant-winning Detroit Tigers, who just managed to nose out second-place Cleveland by one game. The Tigers won ninety games and lost sixty-four for a .584 percentage, the lowest to win an American League flag up to that time.

It was not a great club, but it packed a wallop with such hitters as Hank Greenberg, Charley Gehringer, and the powerful Indian, Rudy York, who had been tried out as a catcher, first baseman, and left fielder and finally stayed on first. He was once described as part Indian and part first baseman.

Heading the pitching staff was the chubby and talkative Bobo Newsom who always referred to himself in the third person. "Bobo will win twenty games this year," Bobo would say, and Bobo sometimes did. He won twenty-one for the Tigers in 1940, his best year, and lost only five.

The Reds, unbowed by the Yankee defeat, repeated as National League champions behind the fine pitching of Paul Derringer, (20–12) and Bucky Walters (22–10), a converted third baseman. Big Ernie Lombardi, the second ranking National League hitter (.319), was out of the Series with a sprained ankle, and the club's second-string catcher, Willard Hershberger, had unaccountably committed suicide in a Boston hotel late in the season. That left only the inexperienced third-string catcher, Bill Baker. It was then that 40-year-old Jimmy Wilson, who had not caught a full season for years and had the status of coach with the Reds, put on his mask and stepped back into the game.

The Series looked like another American League runaway as Bobo Newsom coasted home with a 7–2 win in the first game. He was perhaps inspired by the presence of his father who had come up from South Carolina to watch his boy hurl. The day after the game, as the Reds were winning, 5 to 3, Bobo's father died of a heart attack. (This game, incidentally, was the first National League triumph in the Series since Carl Hubbell beat the Yankees in the fourth game in 1937.)

The Tigers took the next game but the Reds evened up the Series by winning the fourth one. It was Bobo's turn again for the important fifth game and he outdid himself by whitewashing the Reds, 8 to 0. After the contest he tearfully told reporters, "I pitched that one for my Daddy."

The Reds took the sixth game, and in the deciding contest it was

Bobo against Paul Derringer. They had met in the opener, which Bobo won. This time, however, big Paul edged out Bobo, 2 to 1, and the Reds were World Champions. Bobo in the clubhouse was disconsolate.

"Bobo shore woulda liked to win that," drawled the Carolinian.

"For your Daddy?" asked a reporter, scenting a tear-jerking story.

"Naw," said Bobo after a moment of tender reflection. "I wanted to win that one for Bobo."

Gallant old Jimmy Wilson stood out as one of the stars of the Series. He hit .353, fielded perfectly, and stole the only base in the Series .Then he retired and never played another game. Jimmy went out in glory.

The Yankees were not to be held in check very long. They won going away in 1941, helped in great measure by DiMaggio's booming bat. Joe hit safely in fifty-six successive games that season, a record-smashing streak. The Yankees won the pennant — their twelfth — by seventeen games. The season was not without its sorrow for the Yankees, as well as for the entire baseball world. Lou Gehrig died on June 2.

With Leo Durocher at the tiller, the Dodgers staggered home in front of the Cardinals by two games to land their first pennant in twenty-one years. The Lippy One had a well-rounded club which was capable of taking the unbeatable Bombers and might have done so if it had not been for two amazing breaks in fortune. Brooklynites still shake their heads in painful memory of that Series and swear that their beloved Bums should have won it.

It was Fred Fitzsimmons, the ex-Giant, who was the victim of the first break, which came in the pivotal third game. What happened may well have turned the tide of the entire struggle. With the Series standing at a victory apiece, stout Fitz, who was on the mound for the Bums, was pitching his seventh scoreless inning when he was felled by a line drive on the kneecap. Fitz limped painfully off the field and Hugh Casey, who relieved him, was promptly shelled for two runs. That was the ball game, a 2–1 Yankee victory.

On the day following Fitz's mishap came what was surely the borough's darkest hour since the British won the Battle of Brooklyn

Joe DiMaggio's booming bat helped the Yankees to an easy pennant in 1941, when they finished seventeen games ahead of the pack. Joe hit safely in fifty-six straight games that season, a record-smashing streak.

in 1776. That was when Casey, again the relief pitcher but this time doing a fine job, faced Tommy Henrich in the ninth inning with two out and nobody on base. Brooklyn was leading, 4 to 3, and all Casey had to do was to get Tommy out to end the game and tie the Series up at two games apiece.

Casey worked Tommy for two strikes and then fed him a wide breaking curve. Tommy swung and missed. The game was over. Fans started to pour on to the field — but horrors! The ball spurted out of catcher Mickey Owen's glove for a ghastly error and Henrich sped to first base.

The Yankees were still far away from victory, but look who was at the plate: DiMaggio. Joe singled to left, then Keller came up and doubled to right, and two runs whisked over the plate. In the dugout Durocher for the first and only time in his baseball career was stricken mute, too stunned even to whimper. Poor Mickey, who had caught 105 consecutive games without making an error, picked this time to boot one.

Mickey Owen, Brooklyn catcher, made a game-losing error by dropping a third-strike ball in the ninth inning with two out and the Dodgers ahead, 4 to 3. Batter Tommy Henrich took first and the Yankees went on to win.

The game ended in a 7–4 Yankee victory and killed the Bums' chances for good. The next afternoon the Yankees' Tiny Bonham (so nicknamed because he stood 6–2 and scaled 220 pounds) held them to four hits and the Bombers won the final game, 3 to 1.

The world was aflame in 1942, but the American League was the same as ever. The Bombers won another flag without breathing deeply, finishing nine games ahead of the Red Sox. They took it easy all through September as the Cardinals came down the stretch in a furious battle for top honors with the Dodgers. The Cards crushed the Bums in the final meeting of the two clubs in September and finished with 106 games won, the highest total for a National League team since the 1909 Pirates, who won 110.

Playing his first full season that year was a hustling youngster with a marvelous swing named Stan Musial. He played left field. The defensive whiz, Terry Moore, was in center and Country Slaughter, a do-or-die player, was in right. This combination was one of the best fly-chasing trios the game has ever seen. The boys were young, eager, and on fire.

Marty Marion, baseball's Mr. Shortstop, was reaching his peak that year. Big Mort Cooper was the ace of the pitching staff and his brother, Walker, who was also big and strong, did the catching. The Cards were a brilliant bunch of ball players, a truly fine team, full of spirit and unawed by the Bombers.

All the Eastern experts picked the Yankees to pulverize the Cards in the 1942 Series, and after the first game, a 7–4 win for New York, it looked as if they were right. However, the dashing St. Louis youngsters took the second game, 4 to 3, and when the teams met in Yankee Stadium for the rubber match, the chips were down.

The game proved one thing, if nothing else — that it takes more than big bats to win, that a good defense is as important as power at the plate. This was demonstrated with dramatic force in the sixth and seventh innings.

Ernie White of the Cards held a 1–0 lead over the Bombers' Spud Chandler as the two pitchers waged a tight duel. DiMaggio came up in the sixth with one on and sent a screamer between Musial and Moore. It looked like a triple but Stan threw himself to the ground to give the charging Terry Moore all the room he needed. Terry sprinted for the ball, made a diving catch, and then rolled over several times with it safe in his glove. Had he missed, the score surely would have been tied and DiMag might possibly have gone all the way for a homer to put the Bombers ahead. Thus ended the sixth.

In the next inning Joe Gordon led off with a blast to deep left. Stan raced back to the field boxes and took Joe's near-homer right out of the laps of the spectators. Charlie Keller was up next and he powdered the ball, driving it to deep right. Out there was Country Slaughter. He went to the right field screen, clawed his way up to the top of it, then leaped and came down with the ball.

The Yankees could not cope with that kind of fielding and they eventually dropped the Series to the Cards, losing four straight games after their opening victory. Billy Southworth, the Cards' manager, always said that the turning point of the Series hinged on the great catches of his outfielders in the sixth and seventh innings of the third game.

By the time the next season started, the war had taken a heavy toll from all major-league lineups and the game was in the doldrums. The 1943 Yankees, although unrecognizable as the Bombers of the previous year, waltzed home again, as did the Cardinals in the National League. In the Series the Yankees got back at the Cards, winning four games to one, and gave Joe McCarthy his seventh World Championship.

The Cards won their third wartime flag in succession in 1944, as the Yankees' string of pennant victories came to a temporary end. The National League champions did not have to stir out of the city to play this Series, as their opponents were the St. Louis Browns representing the American League for the first and — as things have turned out — the last time. (The Browns moved to Baltimore in 1954 and became the Orioles.)

In the all-St. Louis Series, the Brownies offered feeble opposition and played loose ball. They made ten errors that were good for seven Cardinal runs. The National Leaguers won, four games to two.

It was worse next year, when the Detroit Tigers and the Chicago Cubs clashed in a misadventure that has since become famous as the World's Worst Series. Warren Brown, a Chicago sportswriter, had a good idea of what it was going to be like before the 1945 Series started. Quizzed by the Associated Press in a poll of baseball writers on the subject, "Which team will win?" Brown, who had seen both clubs play during the season, replied: "I don't think either of them can win."

Things started off with a bang in the first inning of the opener when Chicago's Bill Nicholson smashed a long fly to right. Roy Cullenbine, the Tigers' youngest regular at 30 (the Detroit club was known as the "Nine Old Men"), reached the ball just in time to drop it for a triple and let in two runs. Later in the game Doc Cramer, Detroit's 39-year-old center fielder, twice fell down chasing fly balls, and catcher Paul Richards, who was nearing 37, let two pitches get through him. The Cubs won, 9 to 0.

The Tigers evened the Series by taking the next game, 4 to 1, in which old Doc Cramer spent a good part of the afternoon panting after uncaught fly balls. Back came the Cubs next day with a 3–0 win, thanks to their pitcher Claude Passeau, 34, who gave up only one single. As if to remind the 55,000 fans seated in Briggs Stadium that Passeau's fine performance was not at all typical of this Series, Roy Cullenbine on one play forgot to throw the ball home, allowing an astonished Chicago runner to score standing up.

The clubs moved to Chicago for the remaining games where the sloppy fielding and slipshod base running that had characterized the first three contests got worse than ever. In the sixth inning, with Don

Johnson of the Cubs taking a big lead off third and Peanuts Lowery at bat, a sharp grounder was hit to Jimmy Outlaw, 32, the Tigers' third baseman. Johnson was trapped cold —a certain out — but Outlaw for some unknown reason threw the ball to first. Johnson was so bewildered by this that, although he was half way home, he suddenly stopped short and headed back to third. Rudy York, 32, on first for the Tigers, rifled the ball across the diamond to Outlaw. It sailed ten feet over his head and this time Johnson came straight home. A few innings later, Outlaw was picked off third. The Tigers won that one, 4 to 1.

Detroit also won the next game, 8 to 4, but not before a series of zany events had taken place.

Stan Musial as he looked in 1942, when he played his first full season with the St. Louis Cards and helped his team defeat the Yankees in the World Series.

Consider the base running of the Tigers' Hank Greenberg, 34, and second baseman Eddie Mayo, 33. Hank drove a long ball to center and fell flat on his face as he rounded first. He got up in time to make second, however, for his third leg-wearying double of the day. Eddie Mayo didn't do as well when he fell flat rounding first on a hit. He had to scramble back to first.

The ninth inning saw a weird incident when Cullenbine belted a high fly to center where Chicago's Andy Pafko, already playing deep, raced back and leaped into the air. The ball disappeared into the vines that covered the wall at Wrigley field but Pafko did not know this. He thought the ball was on the ground somewhere and he started searching for it furiously. He tore at the shrubbery like a gardener gone mad. He ripped off leaves in quantities, mumbling and cursing. He gave up when the umpire ruled the hit an automatic double.

The comedy of that zany Series seemed to be contagious. It overflowed the ball park and ran past the entrance gates. The Chicago front office that fall had hired the country's most famous gate-crasher, One-Eyed Connelly, as a gate-tender at Wrigley Field. The theory was that Connelly, with years of experience at the art of slipping in free to topnotch sports events around the country, would be the best man possible to spot and halt a fellow-crasher.

Just before the sixth game a slender, bespectacled man appeared at One-Eye's gate. He had neither a ticket nor a pass.

"You can't come in," said Connelly.

"Oh, yes, I can," said the man mildly. "I'm Phil Wrigley."

"Ha!" snorted One-Eye, contempt in his voice at the obvious dodge the man was trying to put over. "You think I'd swallow a line like that? Ha!"

Just then another attendant who recognized Phil Wrigley as the owner of the Cubs came to his rescue. Very soon thereafter Connelly became an ex-gate-tender at Wrigley Field.

Going into the sixth game, the Tigers needed only one more victory to take the Series. They failed to put it across, however, in a game that supplied its allotted share of fantasia and lasted 3 hours and 28 minutes. It went twelve innings. Chuck Hostetler, 40, pinch-hitting for the Tigers in the seventh cost his team a run in a ludicrous exhibition of base running. Chuck got to first on an error and moved to second on an infield out. Doc Cramer than sent a long single to left and Chuck took off for home. Any other runner would have scored easily, but Chuck, in the spirit of that Series, fell down between third and home and got tagged out while he was crawling back to third on all fours.

The Cubs won, 8 to 7, on a twelfth-inning line drive by Stan Hack that went through Greenberg and sent a runner home with the winning tally. Even the official scorers got into the wacky spirit of the Series on that one. At first, they gave Greenberg an error on the play, but later that night they reversed themselves and credited Stan Hack with a double.

After the mirth-provoking fifth and sixth games, the finale was an anti-climax. The Tigers won, 9 to 3, behind the fine pitching of Hal Newhouser, who struck out ten. This brought his one-Series total to twenty-two strikeouts, an all-time high.

When it was over and the Tigers were crowned World Champions, one sportswriter commented, "Most of the Tigers were war veterans and were playing their positions from memory. Some of them didn't remember very well. Thank heavens, though, no one was killed. There were some mighty close calls."

There was nothing zany about the gate receipts or the attendance in this first postwar Series. It produced the first million-and-a-half dollar gate (actually, $1,592,454) and a new attendance record of 333,457.

By 1946 virtually all the players who had seen military service were wearing baseball uniforms and the game began to emerge from the doldrums. There had been some drastic changes on the Yankees. In January, 1945, six years after Ruppert's death, the club was bought by Larry MacPhail, who had run teams in Cincinnati and Brooklyn, Dan Topping, a wealthy young man, and Del Webb, a prosperous contractor from Phoenix, Arizona.

Under the new directorship, Joe McCarthy brought the club home fourth in 1945, the lowest finish in his fifteen years as manager. It was no secret in baseball circles that McCarthy and MacPhail were not hitting it off and few were surprised when Joe quit in May, 1946. He left as the most successful manager in baseball history, winner of eight pennants and seven World Championships in fifteen years. Even though he may have been a mechanical man, a "push-button manager," as some of his critics charged, he made a habit of winning.

Country Slaughter takes the big gamble and wins (1946 Series, Cards vs. Red Sox). The Cardinal outfielder dashed from first all the way home on a single, beat Johnny Pesky's delayed throw to the plate and scored the winning run.

He left with the Yankees in third place, five games behind the Red Sox. That was in May, but the American League standings were the same in September, except that the flag-winning Red Sox had widened the gap to twelve games over the second-place Tigers and were seventeen in front of the Yankees, who ran third.

The dashing Cardinals, without whom the National League would have been hopeless, took their fourth pennant in five years. As usual, few experts gave them much of a chance to win the 1946 Series. The great Ted Williams alone, with his tremendous bat (.406 in 1942 and never below .340 since then) was enough to make the Red Sox the favorites. In addition they had graceful Dom DiMaggio, Joe's brother, Bobby Doerr, hard-hitting Rudy York, and Johnny Pesky, a standout shortstop.

110

The experts apparently had forgotten that the Cards had almost always been great in the Series; there was no American League team, the Yankees included, that they didn't think they could beat.

The St. Louis boys got off to a bad start and found themselves behind, three games to two, but with characteristic gameness they got off the floor and won the next two. The way they scored the winning run in the eighth inning of the final game was in keeping with the Cardinal go-for-broke tradition. The score was 3–3, two out, and Country Slaughter, who had singled, was on first base. The batter, Harry "The Hat" Walker, poked out an ordinary single to center. Every fan knows what happens on a play like that. The batter holds at first and the runner, if he's fast enough, races around second and stops at third.

But Slaughter, running on his own, decided to take the big gamble. He never hesitated for an instant when he came to third. He kept going for the plate. Pesky, at short, took the throw in from the outfield, never thinking that Slaughter would try for such a daring play. He hesitated for a moment, then saw what was happening and threw the ball home frantically.

His peg pulled the catcher some feet off the plate and Slaughter slid home with the run that meant the Series.

Some writers named Pesky as the Series goat, but Ted Williams put in a strong bid for the dubious title. In his only Series, an inept Williams hit five inconsequential singles for a .200 batting average. Stan Musial didn't do much better. He hit only .222. Each of these great hitters, incidentally, won their respective league's Most Valuable Player Award for 1946. Ted hit .342 for the season, Stan batted .365. The Series has a way of humbling the greatest stars.

CHAPTER 9

FIVE STRAIGHT FOR CASEY

(1947–1953)

AFTER THE CARDS had won their sixth World Championship, two of which had been at the expense of the Yankees, their star began to set. They had first come to the fore as a National League power in the nineteen-twenties, largely because the president of the club, Branch Rickey, had originated the baseball farm system (control or ownership of minor-league clubs by a major-league team) and was thus able to supply the Cards with young players of merit who had been seasoned on the St. Louis farm teams. (Rickey's chain store system proved so successful that it was adopted by every club in the majors.)

In 1942, however, Rickey left his St. Louis post and came to Brooklyn, where his genius for building up a baseball organization became evident after the war ended. Even though the Cards had won the Series in 1946, there were many baseball forecasters who thought that their days of glory were about over. They saw the Cards going down and the Bums, under Rickey, coming up.

It worked out pretty much that way. There was still enough of the flaming Cardinal spirit for the team to finish second for three straight years after 1946, but then came a decline and a long pennantless drought. Meantime, the Bums began to climb. They reached the top in 1947 and for the next decade they were the most consistent winners in the National League. They won six pennants, finished second three times and third once.

DODGERS
CLUB HOUSE

KEEP OUT

Jackie Robinson, the majors' first Negro player, broke in with the Dodgers in 1947 and had a brilliant career. He was elected to the Baseball Hall of Fame in 1962.

Rickey laid the foundation that made the Bums' ascension possible, but of far more significance in the story or baseball was his bringing into the majors the first Negro player, thus opening the gates which had always been closed to the colored men. The trail-blazer was Jackie Robinson, a University of California (Los Angeles) graduate who had been one of the country's most versatile athletes in his college days. At U.C.L.A., Jackie was a brilliant halfback with an average of twelve yards a try; he was the leading basketball scorer of the Pacific Coast Conference for two years; he was a broad-jumper on the track team and could do better than twenty-five feet. During the war he served in the Army and became a second lieutenant before receiving his discharge in 1944.

Rickey sincerely felt that the barring of colored players by organized baseball was an abomination and had no place in a democracy. He decided to break the bonds of bigotry by signing a Negro player, but first he had to find one who could face the hardships and the personal abuse that would surely be his until the racial barriers were dissolved. The choice fell upon Jackie Robinson, who was playing shortstop for the all-Negro Kansas City Monarchs in 1945 when Rickey summoned him to his office and asked him if he were willing to try for a berth on the Montreal Royals, a Brooklyn farm team in the International League. If he made good there, explained Rickey, the way would be open for a place on the Dodgers.

The baseball world was electrified by Rickey's announcement that he had signed the 26-year-old Negro to play for Montreal in 1946. That season was a critical one for Robinson, who was being watched closely, and for Rickey's great experiment, but there was no trouble at all. Jackie led the International League in batting with .349 and had the highest fielding average for second basemen. He was immensely popular with the Montreal fans and with his teammates.

The following year (1947) Jackie made his major-league debut as the Bums' regular first baseman, a position that was entirely new to him, and had a fine season. He batted .297, led the league in stolen bases (29), and handled himself well around first. He was named "Rookie of the Year" by the *Sporting News,* baseball's bible, but more important was the fact that his presence was not resented, that the players and the fans accepted him. The trail-blazer had proved himself. Rickey's daring experiment was a success and baseball was no longer limited to members of the white race.

Under the leadership of the Bums' new manager 62-year-old Burt Shotton, the Brooklynites entered the 1947 Series after a tight battle with the Cards for the flag. Shortstop Pee Wee Reese, outfielders Dixie Walker and Pete Reiser, and relief pitcher Hugh Casey were among the veterans left of the Brooklyn players who had lost to the Yankees in 1941.

Pinch-runner Eddie Miksis slides home to score the winning run for the Dodgers on Cookie Lavagetto's two-base smash with two out in the ninth inning (1947 Series). Catcher is Yogi Berra, Yankee star.

The Bombers also had a new manager in 1947. He was Bucky Harris, the ex-Boy Manager of the Senators in the nineteen-twenties, who was now 50 and no longer a boy. After three years without a championship, the Yankees coasted home with a twelve-game margin over the Tigers. Veterans of former Series still on the club included Joe DiMaggio, Tommy Henrich, Phil Rizzuto, and Spud Chandler. Yogi Berra, a newcomer, doubled as catcher and outfielder. Battle-scarred Bobo Newsom at 40 did some pitching. Bobo had made the rounds. He had worn seven other major-league uniforms before donning the pin-striped Yankee flannels in 1947.

It looked like another four-game sweep for the New Yorkers when they took the first two games, but the Bums rallied and won the next two, each by a one-run margin, and the Series turned out to be a nerve-tingler after all.

The fourth game, played in Brooklyn on October 3, had high

moments of drama. There had never been a no-hitter in Series play, but in this game, as Yankee pitcher Floyd Bevens held the Bums hitless inning after inning, it seemed a strong possibility. The husky right-hander had faltered in the fifth inning and had allowed a run on a pair of walks, a sacrifice, and a ground out, but no one had touched him for a hit. Meantime the Bombers had produced two runs, a safe enough margin the way Bevens was going.

In the top half of the ninth it looked as though the Yankees would give him a real lead when they filled the bases with one out, but relief pitcher Hugh Casey, who was called in at this point, retired the side on exactly one pitch. Tommy Henrich bounced the ball back to Hugh, who threw it to the plate for the start of the double play that ended with Henrich out at first.

Now came the hitless Bums to bat in their half of the ninth. Bevens got the first batter out on a fly but walked the next man, center fielder Carl Furillo. The next batter fouled out and now Bevens was within one out of a no-hitter. At this tense point in the drama a cathedral-like hush came over Ebbets Field. This was perhaps the quietest moment in the park's history. Little Al Gionfriddo, a reserve outfielder, was sent in to run for Furillo and he promptly scampered down to second, safe on Yogi's sour throw. Pete Reiser walked and was replaced at first by pinch runner Eddie Miksis.

Up to the plate came pinch hitter Cookie Lavagetto, a .261 hitter that season as a utility infielder. Cookie swung and missed the first ball, then smashed Bevens' second pitch against the right field wall for a double. As the ball caromed off the wall with Henrich after it, the two pinch runners dashed across the plate and the game was over.

Weeping, Bevens walked off the mound. Not only had he been robbed of a no-hitter but he had lost the game by that solitary blow (against eight Yankee hits). It was Cookie's only hit in seven times at bat in the Series and it was the only ball he had hit to right field all season. It was enough to make anybody weep.

After that last-gasp victory, Dodger fans were confident that their boys would now go on to win. The Bums dropped the fifth game, however, but then they snapped right back and won the sixth, thanks to an amazing catch by Al Gionfriddo in left field.

It happened in the second half of the sixth inning, when the Yankees, trailing by three runs, put a pair of runners on base and

DiMaggio came to bat. The Yankee Clipper swung from his heels and sent the ball screaming toward the left field bull pen for what everyone in the Stadium thought was a certain homer. But Gionfriddo sprinted back to deepest left, then turned a split second before he reached the 415-foot marker and, leaping high, stabbed the ball just as it was going over the gate. Hatless, he came down to earth with the ball in his glove. The usually stone-faced and colorless DiMaggio showed some emotion for once by kicking up a cloud of dust in the infield. Little Al's great catch saved the game for the Bums, who won 8 to 6.

The Bombers won the seventh game, 5 to 2, without much effort and presented Bucky Harris with a World Championship in his first year in office. There were some other "firsts" in this Series. It was the first to be televised, the first two-million-dollar gate ($2,021,348), and the first series in which a Negro played. The Dodgers, however, failed to make a first in their quest for a World Championship. As in 1916, 1920, and 1941, they wound up under the table.

Sportswriters had a field day in the fall of 1948 in describing the forthcoming Series as a scalping match, a tomahawk party, tribal warfare, and using similar redskin terminology. The Series was between the only two major-league clubs symbolized by the redman — the Boston Braves and the Cleveland Indians. These teams had never met before and neither had taken a pennant in many a year. The last one the Braves had seen was won by the Stallings' miracle team of 1914. Not since 1920 when Wambsganss made his unassisted triple play had the Indians flown a pennant.

Many fans were wondering if Cleveland would have anything left for the Series after what they had been through that season. It had been the hottest American League race within memory, a three-cornered battle between the Indians, the Yankees, and the Red Sox. As late as September 24, ten days before the end, the three clubs were in a triple tie. At the finish the Indians and the Red Sox were exactly even with the Yankees out of it, but only by two games. The deadlock was broken in an unprecedented playoff game in which the Indians' shortstop-manager, Lou Boudreau, won the contest and the pennant almost by himself with his two homers and two singles in four times at bat. "Never," wrote sports columnist Red Smith, "has any manager managed his team to the pennant like this."

The disputed pick-off attempt at second in the 1948 Series (Cleveland vs. Boston Braves) when runner Phil Masi was declared safe. Here, Lou Boudreau has made the tag and looks for the base umpire's decision.

The Indians had an exceptionally well-balanced, hard hitting team, with three stalwarts on the mound in Bob Lemon (20–14), Gene Bearden (20–7), and the strikeout king, Bob Feller (19–15).

For many years Bob Feller was generally conceded to be baseball's number one pitcher but, like Walter Johnson a generation before, he had never had a chance to pitch a World Series game. Now Bob's chance came after ten years of waiting, in the opening game at Braves Field on October 6, 1948.

It turned out to be a wretched day for him, even though he served up a two-hit masterpiece. He yielded a run, however, and his teammates could not get one for him. They were powerless against the fine pitching of the Braves' Johnny Sain (24–15), who held them to four hits.

The lone run came in the eighth inning after a hotly disputed decision by umpire Bill Stewart on a pickoff attempt by the Indians. Phil Masi, the Braves' catcher, was taking a lead off second when Feller suddenly whirled and threw the ball to Boudreau, who pounced on Masi and tagged him as he slid back to second. There was hardly anyone in the park who thought Masi was safe except umpire Stewart. (The photographs of the play clearly show Boudreau tagging Masi before he regained the bag.) A rhubarb followed the questionable call and Boudreau was still steaming when Tommy Holmes, the Braves' right fielder, stepped up to the plate a few moments later and punched out a single. Tommy drove in Masi who scored the run that meant the game.

Not at all discouraged by that heart-breaker, the Indians pounded out three victories in a row. It was Feller again in the fifth game, which was played in Cleveland on Sunday, October 10, before 86,288 spectators, the greatest crowd in the game's history up to that time.

Air view of the mammoth Cleveland Stadium, where a record crowd of 86,288 spectators saw the fifth game of the Cleveland–Boston Series on October 10, 1948. (This attendance record has since been broken.)

Feller, the two-hit loser of the opener, was eager to win this one and to end the Series. The Indians were the overwhelming choice. Gamblers were giving 3 to 1 on them. It did not take very long for the fans to realize that Feller was 'way off form, nothing like the pitcher who had tossed the first game. He lasted until the seventh, however, when he sadly walked off the mound, having given up eight hits, including two homers, and seven runs. The Braves won, 11 to 5, but they lost the next game and that ended the 1948 Series.

President Dan Topping of the Yankees did not endear himself to the New York fans or to the baseball writers when he announced just before the Series began that Bucky Harris had been fired. The ex-Boy Manager had done a capable job and was well liked by the players as well as by the fans and writers. He had inherited a disorganized club in 1947 and had skillfully guided it to a pennant and a World Championship. In his second season he had been in the race right up to the last two days with a team that was little better than second-rate. For this the personable Bucky had been unceremoniously kicked out by the cold-blooded Yankee management.

Who would replace him? The stunning news was not long in coming. It was to be Casey Stengel. Fans were understandably bewildered. They remembered Casey as a clown, a buffoon who had made them laugh with his antics. It was difficult to think of him in the serious role of manager in the traditionally conservative Yankee organization. His major-league managerial career had indeed been a sorry one. In three years as manager of Brooklyn he had not risen above fifth place. Later, at the helm of the Boston Braves (1938–1943), fifth place was again his high-water mark. He finished seventh four times, sixth once. He did not sound like Yankee material, likable though the old boy was. Casey was 59 when he got his third major-league chance.

The new Yankee pilot made the doubters eat their words as the 1949 season got under way. With a crippled team Casey remained calm, optimistic, and encouraging. He got the most out of everybody and the Yankees stayed on top, or close to it, despite a fantastic total of seventy-one separate injuries. Among the casualties were such key-noters as Tommy Henrich and Joe DiMaggio, who missed the first sixty-five games because of a bad heel.

October 2, 1949, is a date that will long be enshrined in the history of New York City baseball. On that day the Yankees and the

Dodgers concluded the wildest and tightest pennant races in the memory of the most ancient fan by nailing down the championships of the American and National Leagues respectively.

In Yankee Stadium before 68,055 frenzied spectators, the Bombers, who were locked in a tie with the Red Sox, beat the Boston club, 5 to 3, and won the flag. On the same afternoon the Dodgers, who had a precarious one-game lead over the panting Cardinals, played the Philadelphia Phillies. The Dodgers had to win in order to stave off a tie with the Cards, who beat the Cubs on that final day. Win they did, but it took them ten innings to edge out the stubborn Phillies, 9 to 7, and clinch the pennant.

This was the first time since the two major leagues were formed that neither pennant had been decided when the teams took the field for the last scheduled games of the season.

One of the unhappiest men in the land that day was Joe McCarthy, the old Yankee pilot who had been made manager of the Red Sox in 1948. For two years now, Joe had seen his boys finish in a dead heat, only to be eliminated both times in final games. Joe was not one to weather defeat. He quit the Red Sox and the sport for good the following June.

The 1949 Series started off with a pair of pitching duels that reminded oldtimers of the days of Christy Mathewson, Chief Bender, and Three Finger Brown. Don Newcombe, the huge Negro pitcher who had joined the Dodgers a month after the regular season had gone by and had won seventeen games to become the National League's rookie of the year, threw for the Bums. Opposing him was the big Cherokee, Allie Reynolds, with a 17–6 record for the Yankees.

For eight and a half innings the two hurlers held off some of the most dangerous hitters in baseball. Neither allowed a run. Reynolds had given up just two hits in nine innings and Newcombe, as he faced the Yankees in the last half of the ninth, had yielded only four.

Big Don was pitching carefully to Tommy Henrich when the Yankee first baseman-outfielder smote one into the seats for a home run that ended the game and gave the Bombers a 1–0 victory. Don watched the ball sail into the air, then turned and walked off the mound before it dropped into the stands. Not for nothing was the popular Henrich called "Old Reliable" by sportswriters and fans.

The next day it was almost the same thing all over again, except that this time the tables were reversed. Preacher Roe, a tall, skinny southpaw hurler from Ash Flat, Arkansas (population 315), had the Yankees in his hip pocket all afternoon. He held them scoreless and did not walk a man. Brooklyn scored the only run of the game in the second inning when Jackie Robinson doubled to left and came home on a single by first baseman Gil Hodges.

The 1–0 Dodger victory squared the Series and hopes ran high in Brooklyn. This time, after four cracks at the World Championship and four flops, maybe the jinx would at last be broken, thought the Brooklyn faithful. But the Yankees won the next three games and all that the saddened Dodger fans could say was ,"Wait till next year." There was to be no "next year" for the Bums, however. They would have to wait three years before they'd get another shot at the Yankees and the World Championship, and the result — sad to relate — was going to be the same old story.

No team had ever succeeded in the face of greater adversity than the Bombers of 1949, with their seventy-odd disabling injuries. It was a team of great spirit, unlike the usual Yankee clubs of businessmen-ball players that could never win an impassioned national following of the kind attracted to the Dodgers, Cardinals, and Giants. The crippled Yankees, though, stirred the public imagination and inspired an affection such as they had never known before or since.

The jovial Casey Stengel did the Yankee cause no harm. With his rasping voice, big nose, and protruding ears, Casey was a popular figure from the start. The baseball scribes were delighted by him, the fans loved him, and the Yankee higher-ups approved of the way he ran the ball club.

It was an old familiar sight to find the Yankees on top of the American League heap at the end of the 1950 pennant race; it had happened sixteen other times since 1921. But it was a new experience for most fans to acclaim the Phillies as champions of the National League, something that hadn't happened since 1915. The way the Phillies came down to the finish line in a head-to-head battle with the Dodgers left fans gasping.

On September 30, the Whiz Kids, as the youthful Phillies* were called, moved into Ebbets Field for a concluding two-game set with the

* The average age in the regular lineup was 26, which was young enough to merit the nickname.

Bums. They needed but one victory to win the flag. They didn't get it in the first game. The Dodgers knocked them over, 7 to 3, and now on the final day the Phillies had to win or wind up in a tie.

In a critical game such as this finale, a bonehead play, a missed sign, or an error almost always means the difference between defeat and victory, but this time just the opposite was true. The Phillies won the flag because they made one of the worst mistakes that can be made on a ball field. Here is what happened:

The score was 1–1 in the last of the ninth, with Duke Snider, the Bums' center fielder, at bat and pinch runner Cal Abrams on second. Any kind of hit would bring Abrams in and the game would be over. At this point the Phils' shortstop, Granny Hamner, gave the sign for a pickoff play at second. If it worked, Abrams would be out; if it didn't work, at least it would keep him close to the bag and reduce his chances of scoring on a hit.

After giving the sign, Hamner crept toward second. Richie Ashburn, in center field, started moving in to back up the play. Everything was ready for the pickoff — everything except Robin Roberts, the Phillies' fine pitcher, who had missed the sign that had been flashed at him. Robin threw to the plate, instead of to second.

Hamner yelled in horror as the ball left the pitcher's hand and Duke Snider singled to center. Abrams took off for third and the game seemed won. On a hit to center a runner on second has to score and invariably he does, as every fan knows. But because of the pickoff mess, Richie Ashburn was right behind second — about half the field away from where he should have been. In a million-to-one shot, the ball came right to Ashburn. He fielded it and threw it to the plate. Ashburn was noted for his weak arm, but this was easy. Abrams was out by fifteen feet and the Phillies went on to win the game, 4 to 1, in the tenth inning. Robin Roberts thought it was fine to have such an alert fielder behind him.

After the game, Ashburn was praised by the baseball writers for his great throw from "center field," and Roberts was lauded for pitching such a "heady" game. Little did they know that Roberts' boner had won the flag for the Whiz Kids.

"The Philadelphia Whiz Kids," wrote a New York baseball scribe the day after the finale, "will now prepare to play a World Series against men who smoke cigars and chew tobacco."

Smoking and chewing tobacco, the Yankees treated the Whiz Kids as if they were, indeed, kids and spanked them soundly in four straight games. Despite the Phils' chagrin at not being able to salvage at least one game of the 1950 Series, they were by no means disgraced. They lost by only one run in each of the first three games, the scores of which were 1–0, 2–1 and 3–2. Not until the final game of this pitchers' Series was there any show of power and even then the score was low by Yankee standards. The Bombers won that one, 5 to 2, behind the pitching of a 21-year-old rookie named Whitey Ford.

On the whole it was a dull Series, but it was enlivened by the gamble of Eddie Sawyer, the Phils' manager, who surprised everybody by naming Jim Konstanty as his starting pitcher in the first game. Konstanty was baseball's most celebrated relief pitcher. He had set a major-league record by making seventy-four relief appearances during the regular season, but he had not started a game all year. Like the rest of the Phils' pitching staff, Konstanty pitched well enough to win (he allowed only four hits) but he didn't win.

Joe DiMaggio at 35 was beginning to show his age a little. He slipped to .301 for the season — an average that many a big-league outfielder would gladly settle for — but not Joe. Another baseball figure who showed his age that year was Connie Mack who, at 87, announced his retirement from the game.

Although "never" is the longest word in the dictionary and therefore should be used cautiously, it is almost a certainty that baseball will never again see a finish as sensational as that of the Giants in the National League race of 1951. For more than thirty-five years fans had talked about the Miracle Braves of 1914, who came from last place on the Fourth of July to win a flag. Oldtimers were the first to admit that the Giants of 1951 overcame greater odds in their climb to the top than the Braves ever did. More than that, they climaxed the story with one of the most dramatic and exciting baseball games ever played.

It was a good thing that this happened in 1951, for that was a dark time for sports in some fields. It was the year that some twenty basketball players from seven colleges admitted that they had taken bribes to fix games, and it was the year that the Army football team was wiped out by the dismissal of ninety cadets who had violated the

West Point honor code by exchanging information about classroom tests. These scandals left a bad taste in the mouth, but sports fans turned to more pleasant things as the great race of 1951 began to develop.

The Giants were managed by Leo Durocher, who had crossed the river from Brooklyn three years before in midseason. The switch in jobs and uniforms did not faze the Lippy One, even though most Giant fans could not stand him. The traditional Giant-Dodger rivalry was real and bitter, unlike any other in the majors. Durocher was never quite forgiven for having been manager of Brooklyn.

By 1951 Lippy had the team he wanted. He had a red-hot pitching staff, a fiery competitor in Eddie Stanky on second, and a better infield once he brought Whitey Lockman in from left field to play first and Bobby Thomson in from center to play third. Willie Mays, a twenty-year-old rookie of promise, was the new center fielder.

Durocher's kind of team started off the 1951 season with a string of eleven straight losses (the worst in the majors). After that horrible beginning the Giants won a few here and there but no one paid much attention to them. After all, the Bums were securely in first place and could not be moved — or so it seemed on the Fourth of July when they swept a double-header from the Giants and whisked eight and a half games in front.

"We knocked them out," said Charley Dressen, the too talkative Dodger manager. "They'll never bother us again."

On August 11 the Dodgers had a thirteen-and-a-half-game lead over the Giants, and Dressen made no prophetic statements. There was no need for them now. The Bums had the pennant in the bag. There was no panic in Brooklyn when the Giants began to fireball and won sixteen straight. The Dodgers still had a safe six-game lead and it was mid-September with the end of the season in sight. But the Giants kept whittling away as baseball fans across the country cheered them on. On the last Friday of the season Durocher's heroes drew even with the Bums and shared first place with them at the finish two days later.

The rival clubs then staggered into a two-of-three-game playoff.* The New Yorkers won the first but lost the second. Then on October 3 at the Polo Grounds came the big one.

* In the event of a first-place tie in the American League, the championship was decided by a one-game playoff.

Durocher chose Sal Maglie (23–6), his control artist, to take the mound. Ordinarily poison to the Brooks, Sal weakened in the eighth and allowed three runs to come in. When the Giants came to bat in the last half of the ninth they were trailing 4 to 1. Singles by Al Dark and Don Mueller kept Giant rooters in their seats, but hope waned as left fielder Monte Irvin, the team's leading hitter (.312), popped out on a foul. Then Whitey Lockman blasted a double, driving in Al Dark to make the score 4–2.

With men on second and third, Bobby Thomson, a smiling Scot (he was born in Glasgow in 1923), strolled to the plate to face the opportunity of his life. There wasn't a Giant supporter in the land who wouldn't have settled for a single right then and the two runs it would surely have meant.

Bobby looked at a strike and got set for the next pitch. It came in high and fast. He swung and met it squarely. Before unbelieving thousands, the ball sailed upwards and arched into the left field stands for the runs that gave the Giants the game, 5 to 4, and the pennant by one game.

Bobby toured the bases leaping like an antelope. Before he had crossed the plate, ticker tape was streaming down from Wall Street windows and Giant rooters the country over were dancing in the streets. At the Polo Grounds, Eddie Stankey climbed on Durocher's back and bore him to the ground. Baseball writers, emotionless from years of watching spectacular plays, found themselves standing on their seats in the press box. The crowd flooded the field and broke through police lines to get at the big grinning Scot.

Next day the bedazzled Giants woke up to find that while their backs were turned, so to speak, the Yankees had won their third straight pennant in the American League. Durocher's boys were unable to continue their "miracle" drive against the Yankees, who captured the Series in six games for their fourteenth World Championship in eighteen chances. The Giants won two of the first three games, but Casey's Bombers demonstrated their superb class by winning three in a row for the title. In all fairness, however, it must be said that the Giants were hurt by the fact that two of their twenty-three game winners, Sal Maglie and Larry Jansen (23–11), apparently were pitched out as a result of their strenuous labors during the pennant drive. Neither won a game in the Series.

126

Bobby Thomson brings home the flag for the Giants as he crosses the plate after hitting a three-run homer in the ninth inning of the playoff finale with the Dodgers on October 3, 1951.

Two rookies did not fare so well in Series. Willie Mays hit a meager .182 for the Giants and the Yankees' Mickey Mantle batted an even .200. Joe DiMaggio, with .261 for the Series and a new low of .263 for the 1951 season, decided to call it quits. Yankee president Dan Topping told Joe that he would pay him his regular salary of $100,000 if he'd just get in uniform next year and do nothing but pinch-hit now and then. Joe said "No, thanks" and turned in his suit.

One of the many reasons for the continued success of the Yankees is their ability to replace a fading star with a rising one. Babe Ruth had no sooner passed from the scene than up rose Joe DiMaggio, and when he began to fade, along came Mickey Mantle, who, like Ruth and DiMaggio before him, seemed to have about everything: hitting power, speed, grace, agility, and a good arm.

Mickey Mantle, a 200-pound, 6-foot strong boy, played his first full season for the Yankees in 1952 and was the club's top hitter with .311 and its second highest home run producer with twenty-three. A switch hitter, he showed great power from both sides of the plate. Traditionally, switch hitters slug one way and slap the other, but not Mickey. The blond 20-year-old wonder boy who played center field hit twelve homers right-handed and eleven left-handed. He also struck out a lot from either side and when he did he invariably boiled over and kicked the water cooler when he got back to the dugout. One wag in the press box wondered if he kicked it with his right foot or his left.

To the surprise of not many baseball fans, the Dodgers and the Yankees were the pennant winners in 1952. Both races were close but nothing like those of recent years. The Yankees broke the tape two games in front of the challenging Indians and the Bums came home four and a half games ahead of the defending Giants, who had been hurt badly by the loss of outfielders Monte Irvin (a broken leg) and Willie Mays (the United States Army).

The fired-up Dodgers refused to be panicked by the long-ball power of the Yankees and they did everything they could to break their Series jinx in 1952. With rookie pitcher Joe Black on the mound the Bums won the first game, but the Yankees took the next one and that was the way the Series went, with the see-saw aspect continuing all the way. Things looked bright for the Dodgers when Carl Erskine, their steady and courageous hurler, survived a five-run Yankee outburst in the fifth inning of the fifth game and stayed out there all through the eleven-inning contest, which the Brooks finally won, 6 to 5. Now the Series stood three games to two in the Bums' favor and the pressure, for once, was on the Yankees. Could they win the next two?

A battle of home runs (two by the Dodgers' Duke Snider, and one apiece by Yogi Berra and Mickey Mantle) saw the Yankees tie up the Series by winning the sixth game, 3 to 2.

Then came the payoff game. It was a tight, tense battle with Casey juggling half his pitching staff — using Lopat, Reynolds, Raschi, and Kuzava in that order. The Dodgers came within a hair of winning the game on what might have been, and nearly was, the most awful miscue in the annals of the World Series.

It was the seventh inning and the Yankees were leading, 4–2, when the Dodgers loaded the bases. There were two out and Jackie Robinson was at bat. "I shifted over toward right center where I always

Casey Stengel became manager of the Yankees in 1949, won ten flags and seven World Championships in twelve years, and was then fired. Casey piloted the New York Mets in 1962.

played Jackie," Hank Bauer, the then Yankees' right fielder, later recalled. "Jackie took his usual quick swing and the ball went straight up — a pop-up to the first base side of the pitcher's mound. I slapped my glove, happy that we were out of trouble. It was a routine pop-up, usually a sure out.

"I still shudder when I think what almost happened to that 'sure' out," continued Hank, more than ten years after the event. "Joe Collins, our first baseman, lost the ball in the sun. He stood there frozen. Bob Kuzava, our pitcher, didn't move after the ball. Neither did Yogi Berra, our catcher. I couldn't believe it. There were four Dodgers tearing around the bases and nobody was close enough to the ball to wave hello to it.

"From nowhere, Bill Martin, our second baseman, came racing across the infield. Billy charged in like a runaway truck, holding his glove out. He lunged forward the last second and the ball fell into his glove, about six inches off the ground. I still don't know how Billy got there that fast. But we knew that nothing the Dodgers did could keep us from winning."

The Yankees won it, 4 to 2, and Casey had tied the record set by the Bombers of 1936, '37, '38, and '39, who captured the game's highest honors for four consecutive years under Joe McCarthy.

One or two timely hits in the 1952 Series would have meant victory for the Dodgers, but some of their key men were off form. Jackie Robinson, a .308 hitter, faded to .174 in the Series and luckless Gil Hodges, the Brooks' first baseman, went hitless in twenty-one tries, thus capturing the annual goat award without any dispute.

The 1953 edition of the annual Bombers vs. Bums show opened under sunny skies on September 30 at Yankee Stadium. This was the Dodgers' "now-or-never" year. "If they can't win it with this bunch,"

Brooklyn fans were saying, "they probably never will." They had good reason to think that the Series jinx could be shattered. There was Roy Campanella, with 142 runs batted in for a major-league record for catchers; Duke Snider, with his .336 average and forty-two homers; Carl Furillo, in right field, as the National League batting champion at .344; Jackie Robinson with .329 for that season; and Gil Hodges, who had survived his sorry 1952 Series performance and had come back with a .302 average and thirty-one homers.

The hard-hitting Dodgers, who had clubbed their way to an easy pennant victory, continued to wallop the ball all through the Series for an outstanding team average of .300, but — sad to relate — it was not enough to overcome their poor defense (seven errors) and their shaky pitching. Carl Erskine, however, turned in a fine performance in the third game when he fanned fourteen Yankees to break a record set by Howard Ehmke of the A's in 1929.

The slugging star of the 1953 Series was, surprisingly, light-hitting Billy Martin, the Yankees' scrappy second baseman, who broke loose with twelve hits, two of which were homers, for a .500 average. Mickey Mantle, playing an unusual dual role of hero and goat, struck out eight times, including five times in succession, but he made up for it by coming through with a two-run homer to win the second game and a grand-slam home run for the winning edge in the fifth game.

The Yankees were never headed in this Series, but the Dodgers did manage to draw up even with them by winning the third and fourth games after they had dropped the first two. The incredible Yankees then took the next two games and that was all. The World Champions had put Casey Stengel in a special niche in the record books by giving him his fifth straight Series title, something that not even John McGraw, Connie Mack, Miller Huggins, or Joe McCarthy had been able to do before him.

Casey, who had spent nine years in the second division before coming to the Yankees, gave full credit to his players. "A great team," he said, "the greatest I ever managed. We got the best shortstop in Phil Rizzuto and the best second baseman in Billy Martin. We got Yogi Berra, the best catcher, and Mickey Mantle, the best center fielder. The outfield is swell and the pitching is tremendous."

Many baseball writers ranked this team on a par with the great Yankee clubs of 1927 and 1936.

CHAPTER 10

A CRACK IN THE WALL?

(1954–1958)

THE YEAR 1954 was a momentous one in the world of sports. After years of effort, during which many had decided that the feat could never be achieved, the four-minute mile barrier in track was erased by England's Roger Bannister who ran the distance in 3 minutes, 59.4 seconds. And again, after years of effort, during which many baseball fans had become resigned to the belief that the Yankees would never lose, the Cleveland Indians tumbled them from their perch.

Ironically, the Yankees won 103 games that season, the highest total in Casey's six-year reign, and they had more .300 hitters than they had in any year in which they finished first.

No major-league team had ever before won 103 games and placed second. Furthermore, the Yankees led the league in club batting with an average of .268 and they were tied for second place in the fielding averages with the Indians. With all this, and winning more games than he ever had bagged in five pennant-winning years, Casey lost the flag. What was the reason for this startling upset, for the crack in the Yankee wall?

The answer was really quite simple. The Indians had a better team. They won 111 games in 1954, more than any American League team in history, including the 1927 Yankees' 110 victories which are commonly regarded as piled up by the mightiest ball club ever assembled. The Indians did it with a fine pitching staff consisting of two twenty-three-game winners (Bob Lemon and Early Wynn), Mike Garcia (19-8), and Bob Feller (13-3) who, at 35, was no longer a fireballer but a skilled craftsman with a good curve. Their only .300 hitters were Bobby Avila (.341) and Al Rosen (.300), but they had an excellent defensive club, especially in the outfield. It was the "year of atonement," as sportswriters liked to call it.

In the National League it was the Giants' year. From their dreary fifth-place finish in 1953, they had been transformed into a surprise winner by the acquisition of southpaw Johnny Antonelli (21–7) and Willie Mays, who was back from the Army. The wondrous Willie played center field as no Giant had ever played it before him, and topped the league with a .345 batting average. Right behind him were Don Mueller, right fielder, with .342 and Dusty* Rhodes (.341), who was weak defensively as an outfielder and was used mainly as a pinch hitter.

The 1954 Series produced two heroes — Dusty Rhodes and Willie Mays — and they began performing like heroes in the very first game, which was played at the Polo Grounds. The teams were tied at 2–2 in the top of the eighth and the Indians had two runners on when first baseman Vic Wertz, who was to hit .500 in the Series, came to bat. He drove a pitch high and long down the center field alley (the deepest one in the majors) and after it went Willie in full flight, with his back to the infield. Just as Willie was about to crash into the barrier, he caught up with the ball 450 feet from the plate and took it with an over-the-shoulder grab, like a football receiver taking a forward pass. For grace, speed, and exactness, few catches have equaled Willie's. He saved the game.

The score was still tied in the bottom half of the tenth when the Giants came to bat. They had two on when Dusty was called from the bench to pinch hit. Dusty got his opportunity only because of Willie's fabulous catch, but no matter. He got hold of one of Bob Lemon's deliveries and lofted the ball into the right field stands for the winning home run.

Next afternoon at the Polo Grounds, Al Smith, the first man up for the Indians, swung at the first pitch of the game and hit a homer. Johnny Antonelli was the victim. Thereafter, thirteen Indians reached

* All ball players named Rhodes are nicknamed Dusty, it seems. There are four Dusty Rhodes listed in the *Official Encyclopedia of Baseball.*

Wondrous Willie Mays (left) and Dusty Rhodes were the heroes of the 1954 World Series, when the New York Giants defeated the Cleveland Indians in four straight games.

base but none got home. Dusty Rhodes went into the game in the fifth to bat for Monte Irvin and drove in the tying run with a single. Durocher decided to let him stay in. The next time Dusty came up, in the eighth, he hit a homer and that was the game.

It was becoming a habit with Dusty. In Cleveland, in the third game, Dusty again batted for Irvin, this time when the bases were loaded in the third inning. The husky clutch hitter from Alabama rapped out a single on the first pitch to drive in two runs. The Giants won that game, 6 to 2, and the next day they won the fourth, 7 to 4, to become the first National League Club to sweep a Series in four games (without a tie) since the 1914 Miracle Braves.

After the Series, elated National Leaguers asked some questions. Were the Indians' 111 victories merely the reflection of a fairly good team in a terribly weak American League? There was no answer, but one thing was sure: After losing seven straight Series, the National League had at last smashed the American League's domination.

The 1954 Series was staged in each league's largest ball park — the Polo Grounds, with a seating capacity of 55,131, and Cleveland's Municipal Stadium, which seated more than 74,000 and was the largest park in baseball. Consequently, an attendance record was set for a four-game Series (251,507) and it was the most lucrative one in history for the players. A full share for the Giants amounted to $11,147.90 and for the Indians to $6,712.50.

The Brooklyn Dodgers in 1955 ignored the pre-season forecast, which had listed the defending Giants as the favorites to repeat, and got away to an astounding start by winning their first ten games (a major-league record). They were never headed. On September 8 they clinched the flag — the earliest date on which this had ever been done in the National League — and went on to finish thirteen and a half lengths ahead of the Milwaukee Braves (formerly the Boston Braves). The Giants were out of sight in third place and their Dandy Little Manager, as Durocher was derisively called, left for Hollywood.

Meanwhile the Yankees regained the American League championship, the sixth for Casey in his seven years at the helm, and now, here they were again — the Brooks and the Bombers in their sixth meeting for the World Championship. Always a bridesmaid but never a bride, was the Brooklyn story: seven Series, seven losses, and all but one to the Yankees. The lone "outsider" was Cleveland, the Brooks' conquerors in 1920.

On the morning of September 30, 1955, scarcely anyone in the United States gave the Dodgers a chance to win the Series, for they had dropped the first two games to the Yankees. No club had ever come from behind to win after losing the first two in a seven-game Series. There was no joy in Brooklyn that afternoon as the teams faced each other in Ebbets Field in the third game.

On the mound for the Dodgers was blond, blue-eyed Johnny Podres who had an undistinguished 9–10 won-lost record for the season. Manager Walter Alston was using him out of desperation, for his two aces, Don Newcombe (20–5) and Billy Loes (10–4), had failed him in the first two games. Johnny Podres, an upstate New Yorker, was born on September 30, 1932, so the day of his appearance against the Yankees marked his twenty-third birthday. Johnny celebrated it in style. In control all the way, he held the Yankees to seven hits and the Dodgers won, 8 to 3.

That was the start of a three-game rally that astonished the baseball world and brought unlimited joy to Brooklyn. The Yankees squared the Series by taking the sixth game behind the four-hit pitching of Whitey Ford, and then on October 4 in Yankee Stadium came the seventh and deciding contest. Johnny Podres, 23 years and four days old, was given the pitching assignment.

Johnny came close to destruction in the bottom of the third

134

After losing seven Series in seven tries, the Dodgers were finally victorious in 1955, thanks in great part to the fine pitching of Johnny Podres, who twice defeated the Yankees.

inning when, with two out, Rizzuto walked and took second on Martin's single. The Yankees' third baseman, Gil McDougald, came up and worked Podres for the classic three-and-two count. Johnny put the next one over and McDougald, always a dangerous hitter, tapped a little grounder toward third that seemed sure to be a hit because third baseman Don Hoak was playing back and had no chance to field it in time. Rizzuto, scampering down from second, slid into third and the bases were loaded — or were they? No one knew for a moment just what had happened, but soon it was clear. The slowly moving grounder had brushed against Rizzuto's leg as he made his slide and he was out. A batted ball had struck the base runner. The inning was over. Thousands of Brooklyn fans breathed deeply in relief.

The Dodgers scored the first run of the game in the fourth when Gil Hodges, batting with two out and a runner on third, took two called strikes and then broke pitcher Tommy Byrne's heart by hitting a single for the run. They scored again in the sixth and it was 2–0 when the Yankees came to bat in their half of the inning.

Billy Martin opened the inning by walking and Gil McDougald bunted safely to put him on second. With the left-handed batter Yogi Berra at the plate, Sandy Amoros, playing left field, moved well over toward center, which was the proper place to play the Yankee catcher, a consistent right field hitter. With a count of one ball and no strikes, Podres threw a low outside fast ball that Yogi drove high and far down the left field foul line. Yogi took off for first. McDougald, trying to score the tying run, sped for second. Martin went halfway from second toward third and stopped to see if the ball was going fair or foul. Meanwhile the Cuban speedster, Sandy Amoros, ran like a greyhound almost 150 feet across the outfield grass toward the point where the ball was dropping into the left field corner. At the last split second he braked himself on the heel of his left foot and struck out his glove to catch the ball. It plopped in for the first out of the inning. By this time McDougald was a step past second. He saw the catch, turned frantically, and fled back toward first. Amoros, after snaring the ball, spun quickly and rifled it to shortstop Reese, who wheeled and blazed it across the infield to Hodges at first. Hodges caught the perfect throw just in time to double up the sliding McDougald for the second out. Hank Bauer then came to bat and grounded out to end the historic inning.

Amoros' sensational catch was the game-saver, for had the ball fallen safely, the Bombers not only would have tied the score, but Yogi would have reached second or third, putting the potential winning run on base with none out. Pee Wee Reese, however, deserves more than a bow on the play. As captain of the team, the veteran shortstop who had played in five losing Series and who wanted so much to win this one made victory possible with his beautiful relay throw to Gil Hodges for the second out.

In the next inning the Yankees put two men on with two singles, but cool and calm Johnny Podres weathered the crisis and did not give up a run. In the ninth, with victory within his grasp, his strength and speed were overpowering. Skowron, the first Yankee up, tapped back to the mound and Johnny threw him out. Center fielder Bob Cerv raised an easy fly to Amoros. The last man, Elston Howard, took a mighty swing at Johnny's change-up and topped it on the ground, fittingly enough, to Reese, who threw casually to Hodges, and that was it. The Brooklyn Dodgers, after waiting a half century, were at last Champions of the World.

It was like New Year's Eve that night in Brooklyn. The celebrating went on until dawn. The streets were clogged with merry-makers, the restaurants and bars jammed with joyous citizens. Strangers locked arms and paraded singing around the ancient Hotel Bossert, inside which the ball club was celebrating its great victory.

In the far-off Caribbean, where the Dodgers, the first big-league team to break the color line, were hugely popular, thousands marched for hours through the city of St. Thomas in the Virgin Islands. In the Dominican Republic, where the Brooks had once trained, a new baby was named Podres Garcia in honor of the Dodgers' pitching hero. In the Spanish-American press, Sandy Amoros' classic grab was called "El Catch." Indeed, it was quite a victory, this crack in the Yankee wall.

It was another Yankee year in 1956. Mickey Mantle became the first triple-crown champion (batting average, homers, runs batted in) produced in the major league since 1947, when Ted Williams won the title. (Mickey hit .353, clouted fifty-two homers, and batted in 130 runs.) Casey Stengel was voted manager of the year for the fifth time since 1949, and for good reason. His Yankee club, which by his own admission was not as good as several previous ones, including the 1954 team that finished second in his only losing year, made a shambles of the American League race. On May 16 the Yankees moved into first place to stay, and came home nine lengths ahead of the runner-up Indians.

It was not that easy for the Dodgers, who were wrapped in a three-club battle with the Milwaukee Braves and the Cincinnati Reds and did not emerge with the pennant until the last day of the season. Big Don Newcombe, the 6-foot, 4-inch, 230-pound right-hander, made the difference for the Dodgers. The gigantic Negro's twenty-seven regular-season victories gained for him the National League's Most Valuable Player Award and also the Cy Young Memorial Award going to the best pitcher in the majors, which he was. He was also, as it turned out, the goat of the 1956 Series.

Don got his first chance in the second game (the Brooks had won the opener, 6 to 3) but he failed ignobly. He gave up a run in the first inning and in the second he was pelted for five more, including Yogi Berra's grand-slam homer. When Don walked off the mound

Mickey Mantle, one of the long line of Yankee greats, reached the top in 1956, when he won the triple crown (batting average, homers, runs-batted-in). He hit .353, clouted fifty-two homers, and batted in 130 runs.

in the second inning, the Bums were behind, 6 to 0, and it seemed certain that this would add another loss to his bleak, winless World Series pitching record: two losses in 1949, one in 1955.

Then came the Dodgers' half of the second inning, and while the Ebbets Field crowd of 36,217 watched in disbelief and uncontrolled ecstacy, the Bums rallied with six runs off a parade of Yankee pitchers. The Bombers' starting pitcher and, of course, the first one to be yanked by Casey was Don Larsen, a big hard-throwing right-hander who was known to be erratic and easy to rattle. Remember the name. Casey was to take another chance on him before the Series ended.

The slaughter of the Yankees continued all through that second game, during which Casey used seven pitchers. It ended after 3 hours and 26 minutes in a 13–8 Brooklyn triumph. Don Newcomb had been lucky to get out of it without being charged with another loss. The Dodgers were now the winners of the first two games, and the situation was the exact reverse of the previous year's Series when the Yankees took a two-game lead at the start. The same reverse pattern continued. The Dodgers lost the third and fourth contests.

138

With the Series tied at two-all, Casey crossed his fingers and decided to gamble again on big Don Larsen, who matched Newcombe in size (6 feet, 4 inches; 230 pounds) but could not match the other's pitching record. Larsen's 11–5 season was nothing special.

His rival in the fifth game was old Sal Maglie, the veteran ex-Giant who had beaten the Yankees in the opener. Both men pitched flawlessly at the start. Sal retired the first eleven batters, but then Mickey Mantle hit a home run in the fourth inning and Maglie's no-hitter was gone. Interest swung to Don Larsen, for he continued to mow the Bums down, one right after the other, and the scoreboard kept showing no runs, no hits for Brooklyn. The game went to seven innings and then eight and Don Larsen, without once using a wind-up with his delivery, kept on pitching perfect ball.

There was now the possibility of not only a no-hitter but of a perfect game — one in which no runner gets to first base for any reason whatsoever. There had never been a no-hitter in the World Series and there had not been a perfect game in the major leagues for thirty-four years. The extremely rare no-hit, no-run, no-man-reach game in which only twenty-seven batters face a pitcher had occurred only four times in big-league baseball in seventy-five years. But here was Larsen going into the ninth, only three outs from the impossible.

Don Larsen, Yankee hurler, delivers a third-strike pitch to Dodger pinch-hitter, Dale Mitchell, for the final out in the first no-hit, no-run, perfect game in World Series history. Scoreboard tells the story.

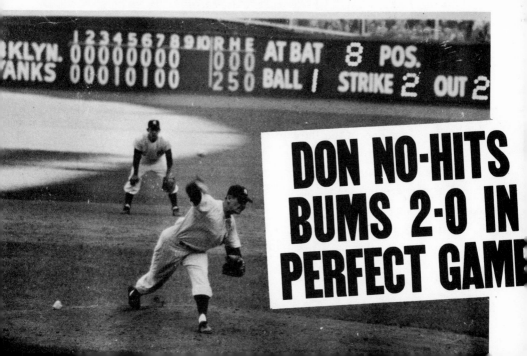

Carl Furillo, the first man up, flied out. Roy Campanella grounded to Billy Martin and was thrown out at first. Now there was one out to go. Dale Mitchell went in to pinch hit for Maglie. Larsen threw him a ball. The second pitch was a called strike, the third a swing and a miss for strike two. Larsen picked up the resin bag, rubbed his hands and threw. The ball was fouled back. He threw again, Mitchell half swung, held up, and it was called strike three. There it was — the perfect game! Yogi churned out to the mound and leaped into Larsen's arms while the Yankee Stadium crowd of 64,519 cheered wildly.

In the locker room after the game, with flashlights blinking and a mob of reporters throwing questions at him, Don tried to answer the best he could. "I started thinking about it in the sixth and seventh and kept saying to myself, 'Help me out, somebody, help me out.' Mickey [Mantle], Gil [McDougald], Andy [Carey], and the others must have heard me. They certainly saved it for me. You gotta have support to come through with this kind of a job."

Still following the reverse pattern of last year's Series, the Brooks came back to take the sixth game. The finale was played in the Yankee Stadium on October 4 and it was Don Newcombe again for the Brooks. No one knew it at the time, but this was the last World Series that the Yankees and the Brooklyn Dodgers would ever play. It was also Don Newcombe's last chance to win a Series game. The big pitcher, great though he was in regular season games, seemed to choke up whenever he was called upon in the Series.

It is doubtful if Don could have won that finale no matter how well he pitched, for Johnny Kucks (18–9) on the mound for the Yankees was superb. He allowed only three hits and blanked the Bums, 9 to 0. Newcombe was his usual shaky self. Yogi Berra belted two homers off him, each with a man on base. He got one in the first inning and one in the third to give the Yankees a 4–0 lead. Manager Walt Alston thought that Don might settle down and let him go out to start the fourth inning. Elston Howard, the first man up, promptly hit one into the seats and now it was 5–0, and that was all for Don. There were not many people in Brooklyn who felt sorry for the Dodger pitching ace, but one man in Washington did. President Eisenhower sent Don a telegram of condolence.

A new face appeared on the World Series scene in 1957 when the Milwaukee Braves won a summer-long struggle against four other National League clubs, each of whom occupied first place at one time or another. The Braves finished with eight games to spare after a dazzling stretch run.

Nothing new was the face that emerged above the pack in the American League as Casey's boys rather quietly stalked off with another flag, their twenty-third. Oddly, the Yankees also finished eight games ahead and bagged their pennant on the same day that the Braves won theirs — September 23.

When the Braves came to Milwaukee in 1953 the entire city gave them a bear-hug welcome, even though they arrived as a seventh-place club with prospects none too bright for the immediate future. The players were lionized by the populace. Capacity crowds turned out to see them play in Milwaukee's County Stadium. Home attendance soared over the 2,000,000 mark the first year (a National League record) and stayed at that level for five years. Milwaukee fans became famous around the league for their fiery partisanship. In County Stadium a long foul hit by a Brave was cheered as if it were a homer, while a great play made by an opposing player was given only perfunctory applause.

The throbbing, noisy enthusiasm of the fans seemed to inspire the Braves, who shot up to second place in their first season and stayed near the top in four successive campaigns. When they finally won the league title, the city was gripped by a wave of baseball hysteria. It gained momentum as the drama of the 1957 Series unfolded.

The Braves' pitching staff was headed by the brilliant Warren Spahn (21–11) who, at 36, had just completed his eighth twenty-victory season, and who was to continue this matchless career until he had won more games than any other left-hander in baseball history. The light-hearted Spahn's bosom friend, roommate, and pitching companion was Lew Burdette (17–9), a former Yankee who had once played briefly under Casey Stengel. The tall, smiling right-hander had good control and a variety of pitches, among them a suspected spitter, but he was at times erratic. He had not yet been admitted to the exclusive twenty-game winners' club.

Backing these moundsmen were such stellar performers as center fielder Hank Aaron (.322), the league's home run king with forty-four; the incomparable veteran Red Schoendienst (.309) who was on second; and third baseman Eddie Mathews (.292) a long-ball hitter with thirty-two homers. This was a solid team, but most baseball experts were saying on the eve of the Series that if the Braves had any hope of beating the Yankees, that hope lay in the remarkable left arm of Warren Spahn.

The Series opened at Yankee Stadium and although Spahn pitched a good game, he was no match for Whitey Ford, who held the Braves to five hits and one run. Whitey deserved the 3–1 Yankee victory. The Milwaukee dressing room was like a tomb after the game. Lew Burdette sat by himself, as depressed as if he, not his roommate, had lost the game. Finally he said to a reporter, "I saw some little things the Yankees did today that I think will help me."

The next day the grim-faced and determined Burdette turned in a solid seven-hitter and beat the Yankees, 4 to 2. Starting with the fourth inning, Lew threw nothing but goose eggs at the straining Bombers. The array of zeroes from Lew's educated arm was going to stretch farther and farther as the Series progressed.

In Milwaukee after a day off for traveling, the Bombers crushed the Braves, 12 to 3, in a Yankee-like slugfest. The defeat was bitter enough for Milwaukee fans, but it was made more so by the appearance in the Yankee lineup of a home-town boy named Tony Kubek, a rookie who played left field. The Milwaukee-born Kubek was the Yankees' big gun that day. He made three hits, two of them homers, and batted in four runs.

While Warren Spahn looked more like himself the next day, he had to go ten innings before gaining a 7–5 win over the Bombers. In this game a bit of shoe polish helped Spahn win his game and it may well have spelled the difference between victory and defeat in the World Championship.

It happened in the home half of the tenth inning when the desperate Braves were trailing by one run and Nippy Jones was sent in to bat for Spahn. Tommy Byrne, the Yankees' fourth pitcher in the game, threw a low one and Nippy hopped around, yelling that he had been hit on the foot. The plate umpire's view had been obstructed and he could not send Nippy to first, but the quick-thinking batter called for the ball and showed the umpire the tell-tale smudge of black on it from the polish of his shoe.

The umpire then waved Nippy to first and the speedy Felix Man-

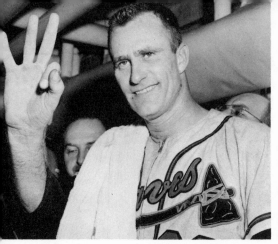

Milwaukee pitcher Lew Burdette humiliated the Yankees in the 1957 Series by beating them three times. Lew started and finished all three games, a feat shared by only four other pitchers since the World Series began.

tilla came in to run for him. Johnny Logan, the Braves' shortstop, smashed a double and Mantilla crossed the plate with the tying run. Eddie Mathews, the next man up, hit a home run to win the game — thanks to a smudge of black shoe polish on a white ball.

With the Series squared at two games apiece, the fifth contest became a big one, especially for the Braves because this was the last one on their home grounds. If they lost it they would have to beat the Bombers two straight in the Yankee Stadium in order to win the Series.

The game was a sizzling pitching duel between Burdette and Ford, two of the greatest competitors in the game. Whitey gave up only six hits to Lew's seven, but the Braves' lanky right-hander was magnificent in the clutch. All afternoon he had the Bombers going after his sinkers and hitting the ball on the ground. No Yankee reached third. Nine more goose eggs were added to the five that Lew had accumulated in the second game for a total of fourteen straight scoreless innings. The Braves won the big one, 1 to 0, on three singles after two were out in the sixth inning.

That should have been Lew's last appearance in 1957, for Bob Buhl (18–7) was scheduled to start the sixth game and try to put an end to the Bombers. If he failed, Warren Spahn was standing by for the finale. Milwaukee's chances looked very bright, indeed. But the Yankees' Bob Turley (13–6) threw a four-hitter to give his team a 3–2 victory. Then, in a dramatic last-minute switch, Lew Burdette got the assignment for the biggest game of all. Spahn was willing and anxious to pitch but he had been weakened by a virus attack, and manager Fred Haney had no choice but to call on Lew, even though the right-hander had had only two days of rest.

143

More than 60,000 fans jammed Yankee Stadium on the afternoon of October 10 to see if the tired but game Burdette was equal to the test. Opposing him was Don Larsen (10–4) who, a year and two days earlier, had pitched the perfect game.

Lew got into a jam right away when leadoff hitter Hank Bauer doubled to left and the dangerous ex-Cardinal, Country Slaughter, came to bat. But Slaughter tapped the ball back to Lew and after the base-running mix-up that followed, both Slaughter and Bauer were standing on second base, glaring at each other. Slaughter was declared out. Lew got Mickey Mantle to dribble one back to the box and gave Yogi an intentional walk. Then Gil McDougald popped up. Hank Bauer died on second.

In the fourth inning the Braves jumped on Larsen and relief pitcher Bobby Shantz (11–5) for four runs, and Lew's task was made easier. He kept mowing the Bombers down in order up to the sixth when two Yankees got on and he began to show signs of tiring. Lew bore down, however, and got out of trouble. His goose-egg run was still intact. In the eighth, after the Braves' catcher, Del Crandall, had homered to make the score 5–0, Lew disposed of Bauer, Slaughter, and Mantle. The Stadium fans, realizing that a great pitching performance was in the making, began rooting for Lew. They cheered his every pitch. They groaned and booed whenever a Yankee got on base. When Yogi popped up in the ninth, he got a bigger hand than if he had homered. McDougald was booed for a slashing single through the middle. Tony Kubek got applause for flying out. There were groans and jeers from every corner of the Stadium when the Yankees filled the bases in the ninth, but when the game suddenly ended with Eddie Mathews' fine stop of a sizzling drive, the Stadium crowd rose to its feet and gave Lew a deafening ovation.

It took some searching through the record books to find a World Series performance that equaled Lew's. Not since Christy Mathewsons's 1905 feat had a pitcher hurled successive shutouts. Matty pitched three shutouts in a row to Lew's two (plus six scoreless innings of his first game), but in one way Burdette's achievement topped the old-timer's, for this was an age of power. The ball Matty threw was as dead as a codfish cake compared to the one Lew used. Disregarding Lew's twenty-four consecutive scoreless innings for the moment, the mere fact that he turned in three complete-game triumphs was a great achievement in itself. Only four other pitchers had started, finished, and won that many games in a best-of-seven Series. It had not been done since Stan Coveleskie of the Indians turned the trick against the Dodgers in 1920, thirty-seven years before. Lew did it before the largest crowds of all time, filling the ball park and watching on TV.

A record attendance of 394,712 was established and some forty million TV viewers all over this country, Canada, and, for the first time, "over the horizon" to *beisbol*-happy Cuba watched Lew's superlative one-man stand against the Bombers.

The 1958 campaign was a cinch for the Yankees. They led the pack from the start and kept going. By August 2 they had a seventeen-game lead, with the remaining seven clubs all under the .500 mark. One New York newspaper listed the daily league standings in two sections, one for New York at the top of the column, the other several spaces down under the bold-type heading, SECOND DIVISION. There, left behind by the Yankees, was the rest of the American League. It was that kind of "race," so lopsided that attendance in the Stadium lagged despite the fact that the Yankees were now the only ball club in town. (The Bums had gone to Los Angeles and the Giants had moved to San Francisco.) Attendance in the American League was off 900,184 from 1957.

The Braves again won the league title, finishing a comfortable eight lengths ahead of the up-and-coming Pittsburgh Pirates.

The way the 1958 Series started, it looked like an early wrap-up for the Braves, and for Lew Burdette (20–10) a replay of his David-and-Goliath act of the previous year. Old reliable Warren Spahn, with a league-leading 22–11 season under his belt, won the first game and had another fine afternoon the next day as he sat on the bench and watched his roommate subdue the Yankees, 13 to 5. This was Lew's fourth straight victory over the Bombers. His scoreless streak ended in the first inning, however, when the Yankees put across one run.

The third game belonged to Hank Bauer, who banged out three of his team's four hits, and drove in all four of its runs for a 4–0 Yankee victory. The Braves rebounded from this setback in impressive fashion. It was Spahn again and he starved the Bombers by serving them a two-hit shutout. With the Braves leading three games to one, the Yankees' chances of taking the Series had shrunk to the vanishing point. Only once before had a team overcome such a deficit, when the Pirates did it in 1925 against the Washington Senators.

AMERICAN LEAGUE

	W.	L.	Pct.	G.B.
New York	74	42	.638	—
SECOND DIVISION				
Chicago	60	55	.522	13½
Boston	57	56	.504	15½
x-Detroit	56	56	.500	16
Cleveland	56	60	.483	18
Baltimore	52	59	.468	19½
x-Kansas City	49	62	.441	22½
Washington	50	64	.439	23
x-Playing night game				

So far ahead of the field were the Yankees in the 1958 league race that one newspaper ran the standings in two divisions, as shown above. This column is dated August 16, 1958.

But the amazing Bombers picked themselves off the floor and began to move. Lew was crushed in the fifth game and then the redoubtable Spahn lost the next one in a ten-inning heart-breaker.

In the finale in Milwaukee, Lew was on the mound, making his third appearance. Opposing him was Don Larsen, who was not in form. The Braves failed to take full advantage of him, however, and scored only one run in the first inning after loading the bases. Then their luck began to run out. In the second inning the Bombers were presented with two gift runs as first baseman Frank Torre made a pair of successive throwing errors on a bunt and a grounder. The Braves tied it up in the sixth when Del Crandall homered with none on, but in the eighth, with two out, the roof fell in on Lew. Yogi doubled and Howard singled him in to break the 2–2 tie. Third baseman Andy Carey also singled and then Bill Skowron clouted a three-run homer to wind up the deciding 6–2 victory.

The Yankees' courageous comeback left Casey speechless and close to tears. In the dressing room after the game, the 68-year-old pilot choked up with emotion as he said that this was his supreme baseball thrill. It was his seventh World Championship in ten years.

New York fans, who usually take their team's victories for granted, let loose for the first time in years and suddenly became vocal. Cheers were heard up and down Broadway, where customers in bars were standing three-deep to watch the final game.

There was no joy in Milwaukee. Wisconsin Avenue, the scene of the city's celebrations, was poised for a big day if the Braves had won. Souvenir vendors were lined along the sidewalks, extra police were on duty to handle the crowds, and mobile radio and TV units were stationed in position to record the rejoicing that never came.

CHAPTER 11

BASEBALL'S NEW LOOK AND THE END OF A DYNASTY

(1959–1964)

IN THE SPRING of 1959 the Yankees were overwhelmingly favored to win their fifth straight pennant. Not only did every baseball expert pick them to repeat but even Bill Veeck, the owner of the contending Chicago White Sox, conceded the flag to New York. In a pre-season magazine article that caused some eyebrow-lifting, Veeck wrote: "I hate to admit this, but we can't beat the Yankees."

The season had hardly started when the Yankees did what so many of their rivals had been praying for: they fell to pieces — quickly, mysteriously, and completely. On May 20 they hit last place. It was the first time the Yankees had been in the cellar in nineteen years and even though they did not dwell there long, they were never a pennant threat. They finished third behind second-place Cleveland, while Bill Veeck's White Sox brought Chicago its first American League flag since the dark year of 1919. The Bombers wound up fifteen games out of first place for their worst finish since 1925.

The Yankees' decline and fall was voted the number one baseball story of 1959 in a poll of sports experts conducted by the United Press International. The experts agreed that the Yankee nose-dive was, indeed, the year's big sports story, but they did not all agree on the reasons for the downfall.

Many things went bad that season for the Yankees. First, Bill Skowron, the muscular first baseman, whose heavy clubbing was the despair of every pitcher in the league, was out with injuries most of the time. He played in only seventy-four games. The next failure on the Yankee list was pitcher Bob Turley who had a miserable 8–11 season, which was a light-year away from his 21–7 record of 1958. Next in line was Mickey Mantle, who had one of those nightmare years: a .285 batting average, thirty-one homers, and a runs-batted-in production of seventy-five.

With the Yankees no longer a menace, the White Sox under manager Al Lopez fought it out with the Indians and finished the race with five games to spare. The Chicago team was a throwback to the kind that used to win pennants in the dead-ball days. They had the best place hitter in years in Nellie (for Nelson) Fox (.306), who hit only two homers all season but who would punch out singles with the accuracy of a sharpshooter. In brilliant Luis Aparicio at short they had the top base runner in the game. Luis led the league in stolen bases for five straight years and reached his highest mark in 1959 with fifty-six thefts. Their star moundsman was 39-year-old Early Wynn (22–10).

In the National League the rise of the seventh-place Los Angeles Dodgers of 1958 to a pennant in 1959 was as remarkable as the collapse of the Yankees. No club had ever before shot up from seventh place to first in one year. In the September stretch thrills piled upon thrills as first the San Francisco Giants seemed to have the pennant wrapped up, only to fold in the final week, when the Milwaukee Braves closed in on the Dodgers and caught them on the last day of the race. The deadlock brought about the third playoff series in National League history. The Dodgers won it in two straight games.

The World Series came to the Pacific Coast for the first time in 1959. Three of the games were played at the Los Angeles Memorial Coliseum, an enormous football and track and field stadium, where the 1932 Olympic Games were held. It was converted into a misshapen baseball field for the use of the transplanted Brooklynites pending construction of their own ball park.

The freak diamond had a 251-foot, left field foul line, the shortest in the majors, which was supplemented by a 42-foot high, 145-foot wide wire mesh fence walling in far left field. This was the infamous "Chinese wall." Fly balls that would have been caught in any other park caromed off the wall and often went for extra base hits.

Dan Parker, sports editor of the *New York Mirror,* was one of the many scribes who were aghast at the weird playing conditions in the Coliseum. Speaking for most baseball fans (outside of Los Angeles), he angrily wrote in his column:

"The only advantage the Coliseum offers for baseball is the financial one. On the other side of the scales, one can list the jig-saw puzzle pattern layout of the field, the hard-baked turf, the blinding sun that makes it difficult for fielders to judge line drives or flies, the type of grass that causes ground balls to bounce treacherously at times, the omnipresent background of white shirts that endangers a player's life when he is trying to pick up the course of a line drive headed straight for him . . . but why go on?

"The fact remains that playing World Series games in this huge football field is as heinous an offense against our National Pastime as trying to decide the world's billiard championship on a table sloped on one side, or contesting the Olympic 100-meter dash on an uphill track paved with brick.

"The conviction of most observers is that this Series has demonstrated more than anything else the alarming extent to which the majors have deteriorated."

Dan Parker was certainly right about the financial advantages of playing in the Coliseum. It was the richest Series in history and all previous attendance records were shattered. The net receipts amounted to $5,628,809.44, including $3,000,000 for the TV and radio rights. The winning shares of $11,231.18 and the losing shares of $7,275.17 were also new highs.

Each game played in the Coliseum set an attendance record, drawing consecutive crowds of 92,394, 92,650, and 92,706 for a total of 277,750. The three games played at Comiskey Park in Chicago drew 143,034 spectators. The grand total of 420,784 was the largest Series attendance of all time.

Outside of the gate receipt records, the 1959 Series did not produce anything special except perhaps for the performance of Ted Kluszewski, a National League castoff, who played first base for the White Sox. Big Klu, a 240-pound giant with muscles to match his size, drove in a total of ten runs to set a record for the most RBI's in a Series. His was a losing cause, however. The Dodgers won, four games to two.

It had taken them fifty-five years to win a World Championship

A record crowd of 92,706 jams the Los Angeles Memorial Coliseum on October 6, 1959 at the fifth game of the World Series between the White Sox and the L.A. Dodgers. White Sox won, 1 to 0.

for Brooklyn, but after moving to the Far West they did it in two years for Los Angeles. There were other oddments: both teams had identical batting averages of .261 and were only one point apart in fielding averages — .983 for the Dodgers, .982 for the White Sox. For the first time in the World Series, no pitcher turned in a complete game.

The Dodgers deserved to win. They played better ball. A Los Angeles woman fan explained with feminine logic why the Dodger victory was inevitable. "Our boys had to beat them," she said, "because of all the nasty things they said about our beautiful Coliseum."

Old Casey Stengel, at seventy-one, was back in business again in 1960. His boys made amends for their third-place finish the year before by presenting him with his tenth pennant in his twelve years as their manager.

In the National League the San Francisco Giants, playing in their new Candlestick Park, were expected to fight it out with the Dodgers for the flag, but they foundered early and stumbled home fifth. The Dodgers were only one notch above them. Totally ignored by baseball seers were the Pittsburgh Pirates, who moved into the lead at the start and held it to finish seven games in front of the Braves. The Cardinals ran third.

It had been a long wait for the Pirates. It was their first pennant in thirty-three years. The last time they made it, the Yankees were the opposition and the Ruth-Gehrig power house rolled over them four straight. The odds-makers saw the Bombers winning again and made them the Series favorites at 7 to 5. That did not bother the Buccaneers, who remembered the pre-season 10–1 odds quoted against their chances of winning the pennant.

For six games the 1960 World Series was a conflict of Yankee power against Pirate pitching and finesse, which to some baseball observers spelled the basic difference between the two leagues in method of play.

The Bombers had power to spare in the first game. They made thirteen hits, seven more than the Pirates got, and they clouted two homers against Pittsburgh's one. But the Pirates' hits were more timely, their pitching was steadier in the clutch, and they made no errors, against two for the Yankees. So the Pirates won, 6 to 4.

The traditional Yankee power was not wasted in the next two games, as it had been in the first. It was hardly more than batting prac-

Pirate Bill Mazeroski bounds joyfully home through a swarm of fans after hitting a Series-winning homer in the bottom of the ninth inning on October 13, 1960, for a 10-9 victory over the Yankees.

151

tice for the Bombers as they gleefully swung from the heels and punished an assortment of Pirate pitchers, to gain their first victory, 16 to 3. In this game, Mickey Mantle hit two homers and drove in five runs. The first homer was a 400-foot line drive, the second a prodigious blast that soared 478 feet and easily cleared the wall in deepest center. It was the first home run in the fifty-one-year history of the Pirates' Forbes Field that a right-handed batter had hit over the center field wall.

The slaughter continued two days later in New York. The Bombers struck with cyclonic force as they flattened the Bucs with a six-run first inning. Mickey Mantle drove in the first two of these runs with his fourteenth Series homer (one short of Babe Ruth's all-time Series record of fifteen). The Yankees got four more runs in the fourth when Bobby Richardson, their slightly built second baseman, hit a grand slammer. This made the score 10–0, and that was how the game ended. The Pirates were powerless at the plate as Whitey Ford held them to four hits — three singles and one two-bagger.

After the game a reporter asked Casey how he accounted for the pair of overwhelming Yankee victories. "Defense," chortled the clownish manager. With the Pirates trailing two games to one and the next two battles scheduled for the Yankee Stadium, the Bombers became 5–1 favorites to take the Series. One Pirate rooter who had stood in line all night with about 300 other fans for bleacher seats, reported that his beard had turned gray during the game.

Just when everybody had written them off, the Bucs clawed their way back in the fourth game with a tense and exciting 3–2 victory. The reason that the Yankees did not put the crusher on the Pirates again was that their three-man powerhouse, Mantle, Berra, and Roger Maris (.283 in his first year as a Yankee), failed to produce. Not a hit rippled off their bats as the ace Pirate pitcher Vern Law (20–9) and relief hurler, Roy Face (10–8), kept them in check.

Next day the Pirates went ahead in the Series, trimming the Yankees, 5 to 2, and again Roy Face came to the rescue with excellent relief pitching.

With their backs to the wall, Casey's boys retaliated in Forbes Field with another lop-sided slugfest. They erupted with seventeen hits and won, 12 to 0, the biggest margin for a shutout in Series history. It was Whitey Ford's second consecutive shutout victory. Bobby Richardson, the 165-pound infielder who was so weak at the plate that he batted eighth in the lineup, unexpectedly crashed through with a pair of triples and drove in three runs, boosting his total to twelve for a Series RBI record. He was to hit .367 for the Series, far above his 1960 season average of .252.

Now it was three games apiece, and as the teams squared off for the big one, Vern Law, who had twice beaten the Yankees, faced Bob Turley, winner of the second game. Neither pitcher was in there at the finish, for things began to happen right away and continued to happen all through the see-saw, titanic struggle.

In the home half of the first inning, with two out and one man on, the Pirates' first baseman, Rocky Nelson, drove a homer over the right field wall to give his team a 2–0 lead. The Bucs picked up two more runs in the second (exit Turley who lasted for only twenty pitches) on three hits, a walk, and an error by Maris.

In the Yankee fifth Bill Skowron hit a homer to narrow Pittsburgh's lead to 4–1. In the next inning the Bombers exploded with a four-run cluster as Richardson singled, Kubek walked (exit Law), Mantle singled, and Berra walloped a home run. The Yankees now led, 5 to 4, but just to make sure of victory, they added two more runs in the eighth on three hits off relief pitcher Face.

It was 7 to 4 when the Pirates came to bat in their half of the eighth, and gloomy was the crowd of 36,683 in Forbes Field. The fans perked up a bit when Gino Cimoli, pinch hitting for Face, singled to right. Then came the break of the game. Center fielder Bill Virdon slashed an apparent double-play grounder at Kubek, but the ball took a bad hop and struck the shortstop in the throat, knocking him stunned to the ground. He was given first aid by the Yankee trainer but he was forced to leave the game.

Dick Groat, the Bucs' fine shortstop and league batting champion with .325, then singled Cimoli home with a shot to left. A sacrifice and a hit cut the Yankees' lead to 7–6 and put Groat on third. Part-time catcher Hal Smith then came to bat and on a low pitch hit a three-run homer over the left field wall to put the Pirates in front, 9 to 7.

That should have been enough for one day, but there was a lot more to come in the final inning. Bobby Richardson, who had been elevated from eighth place in the lineup to the lead-off position, was the first man up in the top half of the ninth. Bobby singled to left center and pinch hitter Dale Long quickly followed with another single that put Richardson on second. Maris popped out behind the plate, but Mantle lined a single to center, scoring Richardson and sending Long to third. Mickey stopped at first. Gil McDougald was sent in to run for Long.

The score was now 9–8, one out, and the Bombers needed but one run to tie the game. They got it, but it was a gift from Rocky Nelson, playing first, who came close to being the Series goat. Yogi Berra started the critical play by grounding sharply down the first base line to Nelson, who made a back-handed stab that spun him around. Rocky stepped on first for the putout on Berra and then looked up, expecting to see Mantle tearing for second. Instead, Mickey dived safely back to first under Rocky's attempted tag, and McDougald crossed the plate with the tying run.

If Nelson had thrown to second after his stop of Berra's grounder, Mickey would have been an easy out, the slow-moving Berra would have been doubled at first, and the game would have ended right there. It would not have been necessary for the Pirates to go to bat in the bottom half of the ninth.

The score was 9–9 when the Pirate second baseman, Bill Mazeroski, came to the plate. Like Bobby Richardson, Mazeroski had been relegated to the eighth spot in the batting order and was not considered a dangerous hitter. A low curve was the safest thing to throw him, according to the Yankee scouting reports on the 24-year-old Mazeroski, but pitcher Ralph Terry offered him a high fast one instead. Maz swung and the ball took off for left field. Out there, Yogi Berra dutifully ran to the wall and gazed at the disappearing ball, high above his head. Rounding second, Maz began leaping like a man going from cloud to cloud. He waved his helmet with each step, danced through a throng of well-wishers at third, and fought his way to the plate through a crowd of back-slappers to score the run that made the Pirates the Champions of the World.

It was the most exciting home run since Bobby Thompson's famed shot in the Giants-Dodgers playoff game in 1951. Baseball Commissioner Ford Frick* summed it up by saying, "The most dramatic finish to a World Series I've ever seen."

* Frick is the third Baseball Commissioner. He was appointed in 1951 and succeeded Albert (Happy) Chandler, who took office in 1945 upon the death of the first Commissioner, Judge K. M. Landis.

In the Yankee dressing room, Mickey Mantle, the strong, shy athlete, sometimes criticized because of his aloofness, sat right down and cried. There wasn't anyone in the room who didn't feel like crying. It was a tough Series to lose for the Yankees. They had outscored the Pirates by twenty-eight runs (55 to 27), outslugged them by thirty-one hits (91 to 60), they had two complete shutouts by Whitey Ford, and they had a fantastic team batting average of .338, the highest in Series history, against the Pirates' .256. Yet they lost.

"I just can't understand it," said Berra in the clubhouse. "We know we're a better ball club. We had great respect for those guys but we just couldn't shake 'em."

Shortly after the Series the Yankees cold-bloodedly announced that Casey's contract with the club would not be renewed. In sports lingo, Casey was fired. Dan Topping, the Yankee president, stated that the club's age limit program was the reason for the change. Casey was 71, at an age when he should retire, said Topping. Most of the sportswriters did not like the move and said so. Casey himself was crushed. He wanted to continue, he was in excellent health and, after all, he had brought ten pennants and seven World Championships to New York in twelve years. No manager before him, not even Joe McCarthy, had been that successful.

"Casey imparted warmth to a cold organization," wrote sports columnist Arthur Daley in the *New York Times*, "and gave it an appeal that it couldn't have bought for millions of dollars. He was priceless.

"From a public relations standpoint the Yankees have done great damage to themselves. . . . It's a shabby way to treat the man who has not only brought them glory but also has given their dynasty firmer footing than it ever had. So long, Case. You gave us twelve unforgettable years."

Baseball expanded in all directions in 1961 to give the game a new look. For sixty years the two major leagues had operated with eight clubs each, but in the spring of the year the American League jumped to ten with the addition of Minneapolis and Los Angeles, while the National League prepared to follow suit in 1962 by returning to New York and putting a club in Houston.

The 1961 season produced a strange situation. The ten-club

American League extended its schedule from the traditional 154 games a season to 162 games, while the eight-club National League, as always, played 154 games.

The addition of eight games threw the American League record book out of kilter and led to some confusion and controversy. Most of it centered around the performance of Roger Maris, the Yankee outfielder with nothing more than a .269 batting average, who hit sixty-one home runs during the regular season, thus topping by one the previously unbeatable mark of sixty set by Babe Ruth in 1927. Was it a record or wasn't it? Not even organized baseball could settle the question to everyone's satisfaction. The answer seemed to be yes and no.

In early September when Maris was close to a record, Baseball Commissioner Ford Frick got nervous and decreed that Roger would not be recognized as having tied or broken the Ruth mark unless he did it within the 154-game limit, as the Babe did. Frick said nothing about many other records that might tumble because of the long schedule, such as most runs batted in, most strikeouts, most stolen bases, most singles, doubles, triples, and so on.

At any rate, Maris failed to break Ruth's record in 154 games. He hit homer No. 59 in the Yankees' 154th game to go to a decision — actually it was game 155 because of one tie. In the eight extra games, the blond, crew-cut North Dakotan hit two more homers. His last one, No. 61, came on October 1, the final day of the season, in Yankee Stadium. True, he had hit more homers in a season than had ever been hit by anyone else.

But was it a real record? Many fans and baseball writers did not think so in view of what Maris had in his favor in addition to the eight extra games. There was no doubt that he was hitting a much livelier ball than Ruth ever saw and in ball parks with shorter fences.

Furthermore, he had faced a greater number of inferior pitchers who would not have been in the American League at all if there were only eight clubs. They would be in the minors. When the league expanded to ten clubs, the two new teams were largely stocked by cast-offs from the original eight clubs. This, of course, meant a general thinning out of pitching talent.

One thing more in Maris' favor — and this is part of baseball's new look along with expansion, franchise changes, the whiplash bat, and the jackrabbit ball — was the shrinking of the strike zone for the benefit of the hitter.

According to the book, a pitch was a strike if it went over the plate between the batter's shoulders and his knees. This was no longer so. Umpires on their own authority had reduced the vertical distance of the strike zone, so that (in the words of retired umpire Babe Pinelli), "It's no longer from shoulder to knee. Nowadays, anything called above the arm pits is not recognized as a strike. The knee means two or three inches above the pants roll." Needless to say, this reduction of the strike area gave the batter an advantage over the pitcher.

In short, baseball became more and more of a hitter's game and less of a pitcher's game in answer to the public clamor for homers. The annual production of home runs in the majors had more than tripled since Ruth's time. This was not because the hitters were three times better than they were in the 1920's. Instead, said critics of the new game, it was perhaps three times easier to hit a homer. In the opinion of many sound baseball men, including Branch Rickey, the Babe playing under 1962 conditions would probably hit more than 150 homers in a 154-game schedule. Rickey said that Roger Maris, or anyone else going for a new home run record, should get 180 in a season to earn justifiable comparison with Babe Ruth.

"A guy who can't hit .270 has no right to break Ruth's record," said Rogers Hornsby, who was admittedly no admirer of the Yankee outfielder.

Be that as it may, the Yankees would not have won the pennant in 1961 for their new manager, Ralph Houk, had it not been for the home-run hitting of Maris and Mantle. Mickey hit fifty-four and might well have topped Roger had not illness forced him out of the lineup in the final weeks of the season. The twin sluggers by no means did it all, however. Outstanding on the team was 32-year-old Whitey Ford, whose reliable left arm registered twenty-five victories for the Yankees and was well worth the $50,000 in salary it earned for its owner.

The Cincinnati Reds, a pre-season second-division choice, were the surprise winners of the National League race, but their hour of triumph was short-lived.

In the ensuing and, as it turned out, not very exciting World Series, they fared poorly against a well-balanced Yankee team and were able to win but one game. Ralph Houk thus became only the third manager in big-league history to win a World Championship in his freshman year at the helm.*

The Bombers won their near-sweep without much help from the injured Mickey Mantle, who appeared in two games and got just one single in six trips to the plate. Roger Maris, perhaps suffering a letdown after his record bid, played every game but got only two hits, one a homer, for a tepid .105 batting average.

Whitey Ford was the Series hero. With two consecutive shutouts over the Pirates in 1960 already to his credit, the incomparable southpaw went on hurling scoreless innings. He started the Bombers on the way by pitching a two-hit, 2–0 victory in the opener at Yankee Stadium. He returned to the mound in the fourth game and broke Babe Ruth's Series shutout record of twenty-nine and two-thirds innings by going five more innings without yielding a run for a total of thirty-two. A foot injury forced him to leave the game in the sixth.

At this point in the history of the modern World Series, counting 1903 as the first one, the American League had won thirty-six times to the National League's twenty-two times. The Yankees, of course, were largely responsible for the lopsided American League victories. Excluding the Series in which the Yankees appeared, the American League in 1961 held a 17 to 15 edge.

Everybody picked the Yankees to win the pennant in 1962 and nobody was wrong. The Bombers did not come home quite as easily as they did the year before, but they did well to win at all. Their pitching staff was shaky (Ford dropped to 17–8), Mantle suffered a series of injuries and was out a lot, and Maris, the home-run terror of 1961, proved to be a flash in the pan with his sickly .256 batting average and thirty-three homers.

At any rate, the Bombers crossed the line five lengths ahead of their pursuers, the Minnesota Twins, and made it two straight for their popular manager, Ralph Houk, who proved again that "nice guys" can and do finish first, even if Lippy Durocher said they can't.

It was a different story in the National League, which expanded to ten clubs with the addition of the New York Mets and the Houston Colts. Everything seemed to happen to the older league in 1962.

* The others: Bucky Harris of the 1924 Washington Senators and Eddie Dyer of the 1946 St. Louis Cardinals.

Roger Maris, Yankee outfielder, hits home run number 61 on October 1, 1961, in final game of the season (game no. 162). A one-season wonder, Maris hit 33 homers in 1962 and batted only .256.

If 1961 was the Year of the Homer, 1962 was the Year of the Steal. Maury Wills, the Dodgers' wiry shortstop, excited fans from coast to coast by stealing 100 bases during the regular season and four more in three post-season playoff games with the San Francisco Giants.*

It was also the year that Casey Stengel returned to the game and piloted the Mets down the path to the subcellar with a record loss of 120 games, and it was the year that the National League ended in a dead heat for the fourth time in its history.

It was the year the Dodgers staged another of their famous nose-dives, only this time it was more unbelievable than ever. With but

*Wills is credited with 104 stolen bases for a major-league record. Ty Cobb's record of 96 steals in 1915 in a 154-game season still stands, however. Actually, Cobb played 156 games that year because there were two ties and they were played over. But Maury Wills stole 97 bases in 156 games, one more than Cobb in the same number of games. Wills, however, did not break Cobb's record, according to the cloudy reasoning of the baseball commissioner. Wills would have to do it in 154 games, was his curious decision. Thus does the extended 162–game season botch up the baseball records of tradition.

Yankee manager Ralph Houk (right) looks over two injured players, relief hurler Luis Arroyo (left) and Mickey Mantle during 1962 season. Houk took over the Bombers in 1961 after Stengel left.

seven days to go before the season's end, the former Brooklynites had a four-game lead over the Giants. The Bums then proceeded to lose ten of thirteen games while the Giants crawled up the ladder and caught them on the last day.

Came the playoff — the fourth for the Bums, who had been involved in all the National League's playoffs* — and the Giants took the first game, 8 to 0. The Dodgers came back with an 8–7 victory that consumed four hours and eighteen minutes. In the deciding game, played before an incredulous Los Angeles crowd of 45,693, the Bums went into the ninth inning leading the Giants, 4 to 2, and then blew it all: the game, the pennant, and the chance to win several thousand dollars apiece in the World Series.

They blew it just as they had in 1951 when Bobby Thomson hit a ninth-inning, three-run homer to give the Giants the flag. This time, though, it wasn't a dramatic homer that beat them. It was an error followed by a bases-loaded walk.

*The other three playoffs: Dodgers vs. the Cardinals, 1946; vs. the Giants, 1951; vs. Milwaukee, 1959 (the Dodgers' only playoff victory).

160

On October 4, the day following the playoff finale, the bone-weary Giants met the Yankees in Candlestick Park, San Francisco, and came tumbling off Cloud Nine. They were shoved off by Whitey Ford who handed them a 6–2 defeat and in so doing set a few records of his own.

It was the blond New Yorker's tenth Series triumph, a record number, and he stretched his scoreless inning streak in Series play to 33⅔. It ended in the second inning with two out when Willie Mays dashed home from third on Jose Pagan's perfect bunt.

After the opener, many fans felt that the Series was going to be another Yankee walkaway but the inspired Giants were not to be downed that easily. Their husky right-hander Jack Sanford (24–7) spun a three-hit shutout in the second game and manager Alvin Dark's boys climbed right back on Cloud Nine and flew to New York.

The 2–0 defeat was a rough one for Yankee Pitcher Ralph Terry (23–12) since he allowed only four hits. He was the American League's top winning pitcher of the season, but the Fates always seemed to be against him in the Series. He had now lost four Series games since 1960 and had yet to win one.

The Yankees took the third game, 3 to 2, on their home grounds, but the Giants came back the next day with a 7–3 crusher to square the Series at two-all. Haller and Hiller, an odd combination of sounds that suggests a song-and-dance act, were the men of distinction in the fourth game.

Tom Haller, the Giants' burly catcher, clouted a two-run homer in the second inning and Chuck Hiller, the slightly built second basemen who had hit only three homers all season, blasted one into the stands with three men aboard in the seventh.

This was the first grand-slam home run ever hit by a National Leaguer in Series history and also the first one hit by a non-Yankee in forty-two years. (In 1920 Cleveland's Elmer Smith hit one against the Dodgers.)

Ralph Terry, the rangy Oklahoman, took the mound for the Yankees in the fifth game and beat his Series jinx at last. His 3–2 victory put the Bombers one-up in games. Ralph was helped mightily by rookie Tom Tresh, the Yankee left-fielder, who broke a 2–2 tie in the eighth by belting a three-run homer.

In the stands a grown man among the 63,165 fans at the Stadium broke down and wept openly as Tom circled the bases. He was 49-year-old Mike Tresh, Tom's father, who had traveled from Michigan to see his son play.

Back to San Francisco went the two clubs, where they sat around for three days waiting for the rain to stop, and when it finally did, for the grounds to dry up. On October 15, five days after the previous game, they met again in Candlestick Park.

The brilliant three-hit pitching of the Giants' Billy Pierce (16–6) beat the Bombers, 5 to 2, and kept the Series alive for the seventh and deciding game. Whitey Ford mislaid his magic wand and at last dropped a Series game. He had won five straight. Next day ended not only the Series but the longest season every played by any team. It was the Giants' 200th game, counting twenty-eight exhibition games, 162 regular season games, three playoff battles, and seven Series games. Every one of the 200 was played with one objective in mind — the winning of the World Series.

The long journey came down to the bottom half of the ninth inning with two men out, Giant runners on second and third, the Yankees ahead by a scant run, and the World Championship still hanging in the balance. A hit, any kind of hit, would give the Giants the title. An out would give it to the Yankees. That is how close it was in the final inning of the 200th game.

Willie McCovey stepped up to the plate to face Ralph Terry, whose fine pitching had held the Giants scoreless. Earlier the huge Giant left-fielder had poled the game's longest shot, a 410–foot triple into right field off Terry, but he was stranded on third when Orlando Cepeda struck out.

McCovey swung on the first pitch. "There it goes!" the crowd roared as the ball arched toward the right-field fence, curving as it went. The wind pushed hard against it and forced it foul.

McCovey took a vicious swipe at the next pitch and met it solidly. For a split second there was no sound anywhere as the ball rifled toward right field. Then in a flash second baseman Bobby Richardson stuck out his glove and caught the wicked liner. The game was over. The Yankees were the Champions of the World.

Just a few inches either way and Bobby could not have gotten his hands on it and the Giants would have scored two runs.

162

It was a good Series and it couldn't have been closer: seven games, tied three time in victories, and the last game a 1–0 squeaker.

The Yankee's great hurler, Whitey Ford, extended his World Series record of consecutive scoreless innings to 33⅔ in the first game of the 1962 Series against the San Francisco Giants. The string ended in the second inning when Willie Mays scored.

There was no question in anyone's mind where the Yankees were going as the 1963 season began. They were going to the top and they were going to stay there. There was no challenger in sight in the otherwise weak 10-club American League.

As expected, the Yankees won going away and finished 10½ games in the lead. And they did it without much help from Maris and Mantle, both of whom were on the injured list most of the time.

Their young flashy infield was the talk of the trade: Joe Pepitone, first; Bobby Richardson, second; Tony Kubek, shortstop; Clete Boyer, third. Richardson, aged 27, was the oldest of the lot.

On the mound were the Yankees' Big Three: Whitey Ford, who had one of his best years (24–7), Jim Bouton (21–7) and Al Downing (13–5). Behind the plate was the master craftsman, Elston Howard, who was awarded the American League's Most Valuable Player trophy for 1963.

Again the National League race was a scorcher. In mid-September the Dodgers were only one game ahead of the surging Cards when the two clubs clashed in St. Louis in a three-game series. The red-hot Cards had won 10 of their previous 20 games and many fans thought that this was going to be another Dodger foldup in the stretch run. But it was the Cards who caved in as manager Walter Alston's men took all three games and went on to finish six lengths ahead of their dazed rivals.

It was the Year of the Pitcher. At a meeting in January, the baseball rules committee had enlarged the strike zone and this gave the pitcher a larger target to shoot at — which, of course, was to his advantage. As a result, batting averages, runs per game and home runs fell off. There was an increase in the membership of the Twenty-Game Winners Club and a noticeable decline in the number of .300 hitters.

The eighth World Series between the Yankees and Dodgers shaped up as a pitcher's battle as never before. Alston had a solid club all down the line and it was topped by the finest pitching staff in baseball. Sanford (Sandy) Koufax and big Don Drysdale were an incomparable pair on the mound and Ron Perranoski was by far the game's best reliever. (He led the majors with a 1.67 earned run average, won 16 games, saved 21 others and lost only three in 69 appearances.)

The six-foot, five-inch Drysdale was a fierce competitor and a consistent winner. Sandy, a late bloomer at 27, was about to reach the

Sandy Koufax, Dodger pitching ace, fires his final pitch in the 1963 Series opener to strike out Harry Bright, Yankee pinch hitter, and set a record of 15 strike-outs.

peak of an amazing career that began slowly and painfully with the Dodgers back in 1955.

For six years he did not get off the bench very much and when he did he lost more games than he won. He had a terrific fast ball but he could not control it.

A sensitive, rather shy young man, Sandy was worried and frustrated until he hearkened to catcher Norm Sherry, who persuaded him to stop throwing so hard and to work more on control, curve balls and change-ups.

In his first six seasons with the Dodgers (1955–1960) his total record was 36–40. After that, under Sherry's wise counseling, plus hours of hard work, Sandy began going places. In 1961 he won 18 games and set a league record of 269 strike-outs. The next year, a more mature and confident Koufax threw two no-hitters and was leading the league in earned-run average (2.06), strike-outs (209) and had a 14–7 record in mid-July, when he was forced to quit because of a rare circulatory ailment in his pitching (left) hand.

Don Drysdale came through with a 25–9 performance that year. But 1963 was Sandy's year. He recovered from his ailment and staged a glorious come-back, appearing in 40 games and finishing with a 25–5 record for a .833 won-lost percentage. His 1.88 earned-run average was the lowest in the National League in 20 years.

The Yankees, as usual, were favored to win the Series, and Whitey Ford was picked to beat Sandy in the first game. The two "greats" collided for the first time in Yankee Stadium before 69,000 fans eager to see which one would outpitch the other — Whitey, the wily veteran, by birth a New Yorker of Irish extraction, or the sensational Sandy, born in Brooklyn to a middle-class Jewish family.

The fans did not have to wait long to find out who was running the show. It was Sandy. With artistry and daring, the lean six-foot, two-inch Brooklynite served up an array of smoking fast balls, wicked curves and baffling change-ups. He struck out six of the first seven Yankees who faced him. In the second inning Ford was blasted for four runs. "Nice game, wasn't it?" beamed a Dodger rooter, knowing that four runs were many more than Sandy would need. In the next inning the Dodgers picked up another run.

Despite his comfortable lead, Sandy kept pouring it on. The Yankees had never seen anything like him in their league. Clete

Boyer was the only Yankee regular who did not strike out at least once during the game. Mantle, Tresh and Kubek whiffed twice and Bobby Richardson, who struck out only 22 times all season (in 630 trips to the plate) fanned three times. Sandy also struck out three pinch hitters.

At last, Tommy Tresh got to him for a two-run homer in the eighth, and the score was 5–2. But that was all for the New Yorkers. Sandy came down to the ninth with two out and 14 strike-outs to his credit. This tied the World Series record made by Dodger hurler Carl Erskine, when he beat the Yankees in Brooklyn ten years before to the very day (October 2, 1953).

The fans knew that if Sandy whiffed the next man a new record would be his. Pinch-hitter Harry Bright stepped up to the plate amid a tumultuous roar from the fans. But it was not for him. The crowd was pulling for Sandy. "A hell of a thing," Harry recalled later. "I wait 17 years to get in a World Series. Then I finally get up there, and 69,000 people are yelling — yelling for me to strike out." And strike out he did, ending the game.

The humiliation of the once-proud Yankees continued the next day when Johnny Podres held them to one run. He made them look like a farm club while his teammates collected four runs. Late in the game an announcement came rumbling over the loud speaker with the news that tickets were on sale for the sixth and seventh games at the Stadium (after the Yankees' return from Los Angeles). It was greeted by guffaws of derisive laughter. Few in the Stadium expected the detonated Bronx Bombers to be alive after their trip to the coast.

After a day off for travel, the Series resumed in the new Dodger Stadium in Chavez Ravine and the Yankees got their first look at Don Drysdale. They could not see him. Pitching superbly, the towering right-hander struck out nine and allowed only three hits for a 1–0 shutout. After three games the Yankees had an emaciated .167 batting average and they had produced a total of three runs. And on the morrow they were going to get Sandy again.

It was not quite the same Sandy the Yankees saw in the first game, but nobody expected him to be that good again. He wasn't, but he was good enough to win the game, although he was actually out-pitched by Whitey Ford, who allowed only two hits, both of them from the bat of Frank Howard, the Dodgers' gigantic right fielder.

Big Don Drysdale (6'5" 190 lbs.), a fierce competitor and consistent winner for the Dodgers for 14 years, shared pitching honors with Sandy Koufax.

In the seventh Mantle came up with one out. He had done miserably at the plate all during the Series — one hit in 13 at bats, which was a fluke bunt attempt that popped into the outfield in the third game. But this time he powdered Sandy's first pitch for a homer and the score was tied, 1–1. It was the first time in the Series that the Yankees had come from behind to gain a tie.

It did not last long, however. In the bottom of the seventh, Jim Gilliam, the Dodgers' third baseman, bounded to Boyer who made a perfect throw to Pepitone, but the Yankee first baseman lost the ball in a sea of white shirts in the stands and Gilliam scampered all the way to third. A long sacrifice fly to Mantle brought him home (standing up) and that was the game.

Sandy allowed six hits, three times as many as Whitey did, but as all fans know, the name of the game is runs and the Dodgers got two for the Yankees' one and were the champions of the world. The first team in history to beat the Yankees four straight in the World

Series did it with 13 players — a surprising feat. Manager Alston used only four pitchers — Koufax, Drysdale, Podres, and relief pitcher Ron Perranoski (for Podres) — and only one alternate, right fielder Ron Fairly.

What caused the collapse of the invincibles and what of their future? Was the great Yankee dynasty nearing the end? Many were the answers offered by baseball buffs and scribes: the Yankees folded in the Series because they were too complacent; they had won too easily in a weak league and had no competitive fire. "They got muscle-bound patting themselves on the back," snorted an ex-Yankee rooter.

As for their future, it looked bleak. The Yankee organization was no longer the efficient machine that had produced so many star-studded championship teams. The brains of the Yankee system, George Weiss, was fired and became general manager of the Mets. The Yankees were standing pat. They were not growing. There were no good rookies in sight to replace their waning stars. Their decline was inevitable.

It was evident as the 1964 season got under way. The Yankees were favored to win the flag again, but a funny thing was happening around the league. For the first time in years they were not scaring anybody. Gone forever was the image of the Yankees as unbeatable.

They were not quite finished, though. In a wild, three-team, lead-swapping battle which saw the Yankees in first place seven times, the White Sox 11 times and the Orioles 12 times, the New Yorkers managed to finish a game ahead of the White Sox and two in front of the Orioles. It was their 29th flag.

The National League race was also three-cornered and even closer. The Cardinals squeaked home on the last day of the season by one game, with the Phillies and Reds in a tie for second place. The Dodgers nose-dived to seventh place, due in part to injuries that side-lined Koufax and Podres, also a plague of batting slumps that visited their best hitters.

Gentlemanly Johnny Keane, manager of the Cards, had a smart and colorful team to pit against the ever-favored Yankees (at 7 to 5) as the Series opened in St. Louis. When Whitey Ford stepped on the mound in the first inning a number of records were immediately entered in the books: it was his 11th World Series (more than any pitcher in history), his 22nd start in the Series, another record, and the eighth time he had pitched the first game, also a record.

Sadly for the Yankees, it was his last Series game. He not only lost (9–5) but he retired with a sore arm and pitched no more that fall. His 10–8 Series record stands as the most games won and lost by a World Series pitcher.

Mel Stottlemyre, a Yankee rookie with only six weeks of major-league pitching experience, beat the Cards, 8 to 3, in the second game, displaying coolness and poise on the mound. Bob Gibson, the Cards' fast-ball artist, was the loser, but he impressed the Yankees with his great speed. They were going to see more of him.

In the third game, played in Yankee Stadium, one more of Babe Ruth's supposedly unbreakable records was shattered when Mantle homered (in the ninth) for the 16th time in Series play. (He would add two more homers in later games against the Cards for a grand total of 18, a record that will surely stand for decades and perhaps forever.) His blow gave the Yankees a 2–1 win in runs, and a 2–1 lead in games.

In the fourth contest the Yankees put three runs across in the first inning and held St. Louis scoreless until the sixth, when Ken Boyer, the Cards' third baseman and older brother of Clete Boyer, who played third for the Yankees, shot one into the stands with the bases loaded. The Boyer boys exchanged nods as Ken rounded third. His jackpot homer gave the Cards a 4–3 win and evened the Series.

It was Stottlemyre and Gibson again in the fifth game, the last one in Yankee Stadium (and the last one there for years to come). The big Cardinal right hander had a 2–0 lead until the ninth, when the Yankees evened the score, but the Cards retaliated in the 10th with three runs and that was the ball game, 5–2.

In St. Louis two days later the traditional Yankee power asserted itself as Mantle and Maris homered on consecutive pitches in the sixth, and Pepitone blasted another one with three men on base in the five-run eighth. The 8–3 Yankee victory squared the Series again and now everything was riding on the seventh and final game.

Once more it was Gibson and Stottlemyre. With only two days of rest, both were weary, but eager. Most fans figured that Gibson, the hard thrower, would be the first to tire. But the Cards got to Mel first and, aided by Yankee miscues, took a three-run lead in the fourth.

They added three more in the next inning. But Mantle homered in the sixth with two on base and cut the Cards' lead in half. Ken Boyer got one run back on a home run in the seventh, making the score 7–3, but brother Clete tagged Gibson for a round-tripper in the ninth (to the delight of both parents of the Boyer boys, who were in the stands) and Phil Linz, substituting for Kubek at short, hit another. This narrowed the Cards' lead to two runs.

With two out, the batter was Bobby Richardson, who had set a Series record by collecting 13 hits. On deck was Mickey Mantle. In this clutch situation, big Bob bore down and retired Richardson on a pop fly, and that was the game and the Series. He had struck out 31 in the 27 innings he pitched, a Series record.

It was the first year that fifth-place teams in both leagues were given a share of the World Series players' pool. It meant $218.81 per man to the Milwaukee Braves of the National League and $195.62 to each player on the Los Angeles club in the American League.

Strange things happened right after the Series that caused a stir in the baseball world: Johnny Keane abruptly resigned as manager of the world champion Cards because of his disapproval of owner "Gussie" Busch's policies. The Yankee organization under the new ownership of the Columbia Broadcasting System, fired Yogi Berra and signed Keane to manage the Yankees.

In the ensuing years the Yankees were to drop out of sight in the American League, their fabulous power gone and their popularity down to the lowest levels.

CHAPTER **12**

MORE EXPANSION
AND THE AMAZIN' METS

TOPSY-TURVY is the name for the unusual 1965 season. The pennant winners were the Dodgers and the Minnesota Twins, both of whom had finished sixth the year before in their respective leagues. Never before had two teams come up so far. At the same time the two 1964 pennant winners went just as far the other way — the Yankees to sixth, the Cards to seventh.

Although the Dodgers were powder-puff hitters, they were favored to beat the Twins because of their superior pitching and aggressive play. The Series opened in Minnesota on a Jewish holiday, which meant that Sandy Koufax could not work, so Don Drysdale was given the starting assignment.

To the horror of all Dodger rooters, big Don was batted out in the third and the Twins won, 8 to 2. Sandy took the mound the next day and again Dodger fans were stunned as their superstar was tagged for two runs in the sixth and lifted for a pinch hitter. The Twins got three more runs and won handily, 5 to 1.

Gloom deeper than any smog hovered over Los Angeles as the games moved there two days later. But to the surprise of everyone, Dodger pitcher Claude Osteen, who had an unimpressive 15–15 season, blanked the Twins with a five-hitter to the tune of 4–0. His victory reversed the tide.

The next day Drysdale made amends for his bad start by pitching a sound game and holding the Twins to five scattered hits and two runs (both homers) while his teammates gathered seven runs for a 7–2 victory.

With the Series at two-all, it was Sandy's turn and again he faced Jim Kaat, his conquerer in the second game. But this time it was the Koufax of old. He was in complete charge all the way and even drove in a run with a single, which was more than the Twins did during the whole game. The Dodgers' bunting, running and base stealing had the Twins in a tizzy. The score was 7–0 and it was the third straight win for Los Angeles.

Back in Minnesota, the Twins' ace pitcher, Jim (Mudcat) Grant (21–7) was chosen to oppose Osteen, who had done so well in his only Series start. But this time the Dodger hurler was below par and he allowed three homers and five runs for a 5–1 shellacking.

Sandy, with but two days of rest had to pitch the big one, with Kaat going for the Twins. The two southpaws staged a thrilling duel that could have gone either way, but Sandy, although shaky at times, had the edge. He allowed only three hits and whitewashed the Twins, 2 to 0.

It was pitching that made the big difference in this Series. The heavy-hitting Twins, who had been blanked only three times in the entire 1965 season, were shut out three times by the Dodgers and had a team batting average of .195, one of the lowest in Series competition.

At long last the National League could do some crowing. For the first time since 1907–1909 the league had won three Series in a row. Furthermore, attendance was soaring in the National, while it was decreasing in the American. Even the lowly Mets, at the bottom of the league for the fourth straight year in 1965 outdrew every club in the American League. And the likeable, even-tempered Walter Alston, known as the Quiet Man, became the first National League manager to win four World Series.

The Quiet Man, however, suffered a severe setback when his boys tangled with the Baltimore Orioles in the 1966 "Hitless World Series."

Baltimore had not seen a pennant since 1896, when the old Orioles won the National League championship. After 1902 the city was without a major-league franchise until 1954, when the St. Louis Browns moved to Baltimore and assumed the old nickname.

The 1966 Series appeared to be a match of power (Baltimore) against pitching (Los Angeles). Baltimore's biggest bat belonged to right fielder Frank Robinson, a National League cast-off, but leader of the American League in batting average (.316), home runs (49) and runs-batted-in (122). First baseman Boog Powell had swatted 34 homers and knocked in 100 runs, and Brooks Robinson, quite possibly the best fielding third baseman of all time, had hit 23 homers.

The Orioles displayed their power very early in the opener at Los Angeles. In the first inning with one man on base, Frank Robinson tagged Don Drysdale for a homer, and the next batter, Brooks Robinson, hit another. Three runs were across before the fans were hardly settled in their seats.

Both teams picked up a run in the second inning and in the third the Dodgers added one, making the score 4–2 in favor of the Orioles.

Mark well that run the Dodgers made in the third inning, for it also made history. It was their last run of the entire Series. The inept Dodgers rolled up an incredible string of goose eggs — 33 consecutive scoreless innings (the last six innings of the opening game and 27 innings in the three games that followed). Needless to say, this was a Series record, as well as several others the Dodgers established as they went down to defeat,·5–2, 6–0, 1–0 and 1–0. Among them: fewest runs (2), fewest hits (17), fewest total bases (23) and lowest club batting overage (.142). To add to the nightmare, the Dodgers made six errors in the second game, three of them in one inning by center fielder Willie Davis who dropped two flies and threw the ball into the Dodger dugout as two runners scored. Meanwhile, the Orioles rubbed it in by playing errorless ball in all four games.

In the debacle, the Dodgers' magnificent pair, Drysdale and Koufax, did not finish a game. Sandy dropped his only start; Don was lifted twice. After the Series Sandy announced his retirement. The severe arthritis in his pitching arm threatened to cripple him if he continued.

This was the first Series played under the new Commissioner of Baseball, William D. Eckert, a retired Air Force general, who succeeded Ford Frick (and would himself be replaced by lawyer Bowie Kuhn in 1969).

On the morning of September 7, 1967, after five months and 698 games of baseball four teams were tied for the lead in the American League. They were: Chicago, Minnesota, Detroit and Boston (up

The Robinson boys, Frank (left) and Brooks, Baltimore's famous pair, demonstrate their one-two punch after striking successive home runs in the first inning of the opening game of the 1966 Series at Los Angeles.

from ninth place the year before). Never before had four clubs been deadlocked that late in the season.

They clung together almost to the end. Chicago wavered in the last week but on the final day the other three clubs were so close that any one of them could have won the flag. It was the Red Sox who made it by whipping the Twins in the finale, while Detroit lost to California. Boston's big gun was Carl (Yaz) Yastrzemski, whose bat made the difference in the stretch. In the last game he made four straight hits. The slugging left fielder won the Triple Crown with a .326 batting average, 44 homers and 121 RBI's.

The Cards breezed to the National League flag and were well rested for the opener in Boston, three days after the season ended. The weary Red Sox faced Bob Gibson who hurled the Cards to a 2–1 victory, allowing only six hits. It was left fielder Lou Brock who scored the winning run in the seventh, when he made his fourth hit of the game, a single, stole second (for the second time) and moved to third and home on two infield outs. Lou Brock and Bob Gibson set the pattern in this game for their brilliant play throughout the Series.

Yaz went hitless and was so disgusted with himself that he kept his uniform on after the game and spent a half-hour in the batting cage. "I'll get three hits tomorrow," he said.

Yaz made good his promise the next day. Two of the hits were homers, as the Bosox won, 5–0, behind the almost perfect pitching of Jim Lonborg. The 25-year-old right-hander had a no-hitter going until the eighth inning with two out, when second baseman Julian Javier rapped him for a two-bagger. It was the Cards' only hit.

Speedy Lou Brock got going again in the third game, which was played in St. Louis. He hit a triple in the first inning and came home on a single by center fielder Curt Flood. In the sixth he beat out a bunt, raced to third on a wild pickoff throw, then came in on a single by ex-Yankee Roger Maris. The Cards won, 5 to 2.

Next day Bob Gibson and Lou Brock were at it again. Lou boosted his Series average to .500 with a double and a single, and also

Triple Crown winner Carl (Yaz) Yastrzemski was Boston's big gun in 1967, when he batted .326, hit 44 homers and drove in 121 runs. Without him the Red Sox would not have won the pennant.

Lou Brock of the Cardinals loses his cap as he steals third base on Red Sox pitcher, Jim Lonborg, in the seventh game of the 1967 Series. A minute before he had stolen second. He made a Series record by stealing seven bases, and also hit .414.

stole another base. Bob proved to be better than he was in the first game, allowing only five hits in a 6–0 victory. The Cards were now within one win of the world championship.

However, the Red Sox were not yet finished. In the fifth game their lone ace hurler, Jim Lonborg, was superb, holding the Cards to three hits and one run, while Boston scored three times.

In Boston the "dead" team came to life again and exploded with a home-run attack that buried the Cards, 8–4, thus forcing a seventh game.

Now came the Great Confrontation — Gibson and Lonborg, the two great ones, each the winner of two games in the Series. Bob had the advantage with three days of rest, while Jim had only two days' respite and this may have been the cause of his downfall. The Cards got to him for seven runs before he was lifted in the sixth inning. Gibson squelched the Red Sox, yielding only three hits and two runs, and hit a home run to boot. Brock got two hits and ran wild again. He singled in the fifth, then stole second and third. In the ninth he walked and stole second. It was his seventh stolen base in the Series, thus breaking the record of six that had been on the books since 1907. He also hit a resounding .414.

By defeating the Red Sox, 7 to 2, Bob Gibson joined an exclusive group of six other pitchers who had completed three winning games in a single Series.

The 1968 season was one of the dullest within memory. The character of the game was changing. It was slowing down to a turtle crawl. Interminable three-hour games were common as platoons of pitchers paraded to the mound. Pitching dominated the game as never before. Strikeouts prevailed, hitting and run production fell off, and so did attendance. (Yastrzemski won the American League batting championship with .301, the lowest percentage in history.)

The league races were virtually settled by mid-summer. The Cards and the Detroit Tigers led their respective leagues almost from the start and finished out of sight. Detroit was the fifth different team to win the American League flag in as many years. It was the Tigers' first World Series in 23 years.

Their big star was the much-talked-about Dennis (Denny) Mc-Lain, a brash and cocky 24-year-old pitcher who won 31 games in the regular season and lost six. He was the first 31-game winner since Lefty Grove in 1931. The Tigers believed that Denny would take care of Bob Gibson in the Series. And Tiger fans hoped that likeable outfielder Al Kaline would make a good showing. He had been a reliable .300 hitter for Detroit for 16 seasons but had never played in a Series. This one meant a lot to him.

"I want to humiliate the Cardinals," said Denny McLain as he took the mound in the opener. Bob Gibson, whose earned-run average of 1.12 was the lowest ever in the National League, was his opponent. Here was another Great Confrontation, a duel that would perhaps settle the question: who is the best pitcher in baseball?

There was no question that day in St. Louis. Denny had nothing; Bob had everything that could be asked of a pitcher. After giving up three runs, Denny went to the showers in the sixth. Bob stayed on, striking out man after man and holding the Tigers scoreless. When he started the ninth he had allowed but five hits and had struck out 14. One more and Koufax's record would be tied. Bob fanned Al Kaline, then for good measure struck out the next two for a record of 17.

Bob Gibson, the Cardinals' great pitcher, won seven consecutive World Series games and completed every one (1964, 1967 and 1968). He also won the Cy Young Award in 1970 for the second time, and is one of only three to do this. The other two are Denny McLain and Sandy Koufax.

179

Lou Brock's homer in the seventh made the score 4–0, and that was the final tally.

Mickey Lolich, the Tigers' southpaw who had been overshadowed by McLain all season, had his day in the next game. He blanked the Cards and got two hits. One was a home run, the first he had ever hit in his entire 15-year professional baseball career, including the minor leagues. The Tigers won easily, 8 to 1.

The Cards showed their muscles in the third game, in Tiger Stadium, with a 13-hit attack that included two homers and a pair of doubles for a 7–3 triumph. Lou Brock got three hits and stole three bases.

It was even easier for the Cards the next day as the Gibson and Brock wrecking crew went to work at the expense of Denny McLain, who did not last three full innings and gave up six hits and four runs. He also made a costly error.

Bob held the Tigers well in check and beat them, 10 to 1. He hit a homer, his second in Series competition, which was a record for a pitcher, and broke another record by winning his seventh straight complete game.

Lou Brock dynamited the Tigers with a homer (off McLain), a triple, a double and his seventh stolen base of the Series.

To the surprise of many, Mickey Lolich, after giving up three runs in the first inning of the fifth game, weathered the assault, allowed no more runs and went on to win, 5 to 3. The clubs moved to St. Louis with the Cards having a 3–2 edge in games.

McLain at last lived up to expectations in the sixth contest as the Tigers butchered seven St. Louis pitchers, scored 10 runs in the third inning and won, 13 to 1.

The Series came down to the seventh game, but the Cards were not worried, not with Bob Gibson in good shape after three days' rest, which was one more than Mickey Lolich would have.

Both pitchers had won two games and were facing each other for the first time. For six innings they locked horns in a scoreless battle, but the breakthrough finally came in the seventh when Gibson, after retiring the first two batters, got tagged for two singles. Then outfielder Jim Northrup came up and lined one to center field. Curt Flood, the best defensive outfielder in the National League, came in for the ball, lost it momentarily, turned and slipped, and the ball sailed over

Al Kaline, reliable Detroit outfielder for 16 years (1953–1968) finally got his chance to play in the Series in 1968, when the Tigers met the Cards. He made the most of it by batting .379 and helping his club win the world championship.

his head. The two base runners scored and that was the ball game. Gibson hung on to the end, but lost, 4 to 1.

Three-game winner Mickey Lolich was voted the Series outstanding performer, but right behind him was the old pro, Al Kaline, who made the most of his only Series by batting .379 and playing a fine defensive game.

Professional baseball celebrated its centennial in 1969, dating its origin to the Cincinnati Red Stockings of 1869, the first team to turn pro. It was a year of great significance in baseball's history. The entire structure of the game was changed.

In another wave of expansion, the major leagues increased their membership from 20 clubs to 24 (12 in each league) and in an unprecedented move each league was split into two six-team divisions (Eastern and Western). Thus, no team could finish the season lower than sixth place in the standings.

At the end of the regular season the Eastern and Western divisional leaders of each league would meet in a set of best-of-five playoff games for the pennant. The two league champions would then be matched, as before, in the traditional best-of-seven World Series. There was no change in the Series, but the method of determining the league championship was vastly different.

In response to the public clamor for more action in the slow-paced game, the rules makers ended the Era of the Pitcher by shrinking the strike zone down to its 1962 proportions and also lowering the height of the pitcher's mound from 15 inches to 10. The pitchers could no longer stifle the batters and as a result hitting immediately improved, more men got on base and more runs were scored. (In 1968 only six men in the big leagues batted .300 or better; by 1970 the number had soared to 39.)

For all of the changes in the game, the biggest thing that happened in baseball that year (and perhaps in any year) was the rise to glory of the New York Mets.

The National League club came into being in 1962 due to the efforts and financial backing of Joan Whitney Payson (Mrs. Charles S.), a noted sportswoman, and it immediately established many records — all on the negative side. It was a joke team, perhaps the worst on record, but it was surprisingly popular and even outdrew the Yankees. The "Amazin' Mets," as they were called by their host of loyal rooters, finished 10th five times and ninth twice in the first seven years of their existence, while losing a total of 737 games.

Then, in 1969 under the management of Gil Hodges, who had succeeded Casey Stengel the year before, their young pitchers got going, the team jelled and the Mets did the impossible. They "out-miracled" all other miracle teams of the past.

The climb started on August 14, when the Mets were 9½ games behind the Cubs and 8½ in back of the second-place Cards in the Eastern Division. Suddenly they began to roll. They crushed the two leading clubs and went on a wild winning spree. On September 10 they reached the top for the first time in their lives. They not only stayed there, they kept on going and finished the season eight games ahead of the Cubs.

Their momentum continued. They demolished the Atlanta Braves, winners of the Western Division, in three straight playoff games and the National League pennant was theirs.

In the American League Baltimore made a shambles of the Eastern Division by finishing 19 games in front of the pack. The Orioles then obliterated the Minnesota Twins, the Western Division champions, without losing a game.

The Orioles were heavily favored to capture the Series, but the Mets were unconcerned about the dope sheets. After all, in the spring the Las Vegas bookies had offered 100 to 1 that the Mets would not win the pennant.

Tom Seaver, the Mets' ace pitcher (25–7) started against Baltimore's best, Mike Cuellar, a Cuban southpaw who had a 23–11 season. Mike was the better of the two that day as several of the weaker Oriole bats put an end to the 25-year-old Seaver's 11-game winning streak with a 4–1 victory. Even so Baltimore's big three, Boog Powell and the two Robinson boys, did nothing at the plate — an ominous sign, indeed.

The Orioles were 4 to 1 to win the Series as the teams faced each other in the second game at Baltimore. But young (24 years)

Tom Seaver, the New York Mets' brilliant pitcher, led the majors in 1969 with a 25–7 record and helped his team win the pennant and the Series in a history-making upset.

Tommie Agee, the Mets' center fielder, snares a screamer to right center with a diving grab to end an inning, with three Orioles on base. It was his second great catch in the third game of the 1969 Series. He topped it by hitting a homer.

Jerry Koosman in his second full season with the Mets smothered the Oriole bats, allowing only two hits and a single run as the New Yorkers won, 2 to 1, and evened the Series. Again the bats of the big three were silent.

It is highly doubtful that anyone who saw the third game in Shea Stadium in New York will ever forget what Tommie Agee, the Mets' center fielder, did that afternoon. Tommie began his one-man show in the first inning by blasting a homer off Jim Palmer, the Oriole starter. In the fourth with two Baltimore runners on base and two out Tommie sprinted to the 396-foot marker in left center and made an unbelievable back-handed, finger-tip catch against the wall of catcher Elrod Herrick's towering smash. In the seventh with two out and the bases loaded, Baltimore's Paul Blair lined a hard drive to right center that was going for a triple until Tommie snared it with a headlong diving catch. Either play of his is ranked with the most sensational catches in Series history. By himself Tommie saved six runs. Gary Gentry, the Mets' rookie pitcher, was credited with the 5–0 win.

184

Tom Seaver redeemed himself in the fourth game by pitching a 6-hit game and giving up one run, while the Mets scored two for their third victory in the Series. It took them 10 innings to do it, however. Ron Swoboda, the Met's right fielder, saved the game by making a diving grab of Brooks Robinson's line drive in the ninth inning. The Amazin' Mets were living up to their name.

It looked like Baltimore's day in the third inning of the fifth game when Jerry Koosman was clobbered for two homers and three runs, but the cool left-hander pitched scoreless ball after that, and by the seventh inning the Mets had drawn even. In the next inning they clinched it on doubles by left fielder Cleon Jones and Ron Swoboda, and two Baltimore errors. The final score was 5–3 and the Mets were the World Champions sitting on Mount Olympus after seven long years in the lower regions.

Big blasé New York went out of its mind in unbridled ecstasy. In the streets total strangers embraced, 1254 tons of ticker tape and

New York went wild over the Mets' victory and celebrated by pouring 1254 tons of paper from windows all over the city. *Below*, Wall Street after the celebration.

torn paper cascaded down from skyscrapers (according to TRUE magazine), auto horns blasted incessantly, crowds snake-danced on Broadway and teachers dismissed their classes so the young could join the celebration. President Nixon called up Joan Payson and congratulated her and the team.

Across the nation millions cheered, for the Mets had won the hearts of the American people as no other team ever had.

"How did the Mets do it?" was the question everybody was asking. To baseball men the answer was simple: good pitching, hitting when it counted and solid fielding.

They held the heavy-hitting Orioles to a lowly .146 team average and squelched the big three. Boog Powell got five hits but they were all singles. Frank Robinson hit .188 and Brooks Robinson went 1 for 19 and averaged .053. The old baseball adage, "Good pitching will always stop good hitting," was proved correct in the 1969 Series. And it was to be proved so again in the next Series.

Alas! the Mets were no longer Amazin' in 1970. They were, in fact, mediocre, due in great part to the failure of Tom Seaver's golden arm in the second half of the season. After winning 14 games and losing five in the first half, Tom did a complete turnabout. He won only four more games and finished the year with a lackluster 18–12 record. As he went, so went the Mets.

They finished third, one game behind the Cubs and six games below the first-place Pirates.

In the West Division of the National League, the Cincinnati Reds coasted home, 14½ games ahead of the Dodgers. The Big Red Machine, as the powerful club was called, boasted four .300 hitters and the game's outstanding catcher, Johnny Bench, a 22-year-old slugger with one of the best arms ever seen. Johnny batted .293 and led the majors in homers (45) and RBI's (148).

"I manage the best team in baseball," exulted Sparky Anderson, pilot of the Reds, as his boys set down the Pirates without losing a game in the divisional fight for the league championship.

Some baseball critics detected a weakness in the club, however, as the season drew to a close. The Reds had won 70 of their first 100 games (a most impressive record) but could win only 32 out of the next 62 games — a drop in winning percentage from .700 to barely over .500. Why the decline? One answer was their pitching. Their two most dependable moundsmen, Wayne Simpson (14–3) and Jim Merritt (20–12) were out with injuries in the second half of the season and were not expected to play in the Series.

The American League East was another runaway for the Orioles, who finished 15 games in front of the second-place Yankees. They had the best pitching staff in baseball. It revolved around their three 20-game winners: Mike Cuellar (24–8), Jim Palmer (20–10) and Dave McNally (24–9), who were known in that order as Mr. Calm, Mr. Cool and Mr. Collected.

The Minnesota Twins again won the West Division title and again clashed with the Orioles for the pennant. It was a repeat performance of their 1969 playoff. The Twins were obliterated in a three-game sweep. These victories extended the Orioles' winning streak to 14, as they had won the last 11 games of the regular season.

The first Series to be played on artificial grass opened in Cincinnati's new Riverfront Stadium, and the pattern of what was to come was immediately established. The Reds got out in front with a three-run lead, but the Orioles slammed their pitchers and went on to win, 4 to 3, making the "impossible" play whenever a Cincinnati rally threatened. So it was in the first game and also in the second, which the Orioles won, 6 to 5, after overcoming a four-run lead.

Most of the impossible plays were made by Brooks Robinson, who staged the most dazzling one-man performance with bat and glove ever seen in a Series. What he did all through the five-game set was almost beyond belief. A capsule account of the 33-year-old third baseman's deeds is the story of the Series. (Remember, this is the same man who got one hit in 19 times at bat in the 1969 Series.)

In the first game he made three spectacular stops, one of them a lunging backhanded grab and throw from 25 feet behind third base and in foul ground to put out Lee May, the Reds' first baseman. He hit a game-winning homer in the seventh to break a tie and give his team the 4–3 victory.

The next day the Human Vacuum Cleaner, as he was called because he sucked up everything in sight, robbed May of another hard smash with a diving grab to start a double play and end a rally. He drove in the tying run with a single and scored the deciding run in the 6–5 win.

Brooks Robinson connects for a homer off Cincinnati's Gary Nolan in the second inning of the fourth game in the 1970 Series. The catcher is Johnny Bench. This was Robinson's second homer in the Series, in which he batted .429.

In the third game (at Baltimore) Brooks made a diving, end-of-the-webbing catch of Johnny Bench's low liner to his left in the sixth inning. (By this time the admiring Reds were calling him "Mr. Hoover, president of the Hoover Vacuum Cleaner Company.") At bat Brooks drove in two first-inning runs with the first of his two doubles to start a 9–3 triumph over the Reds.

In the fourth game (the only one the Reds won in the Series) he handled only one routine chance, but he had a perfect day at the plate with four hits, one of them a homer, and drove in two runs.

The Reds won, 6 to 5, and ended Baltimore's string of 17 straight victories. Before this game was over *Sport Magazine* named Brooks the Most Valuable Player of the Series and gave him a car.

In the fifth and final game, which the Orioles won, 9 to 3, Brooks again did the impossible by diving across the foul line to stab Bench's ninth inning smash. He hit a single to post a 9-for-21 Series record and a .429 average. In the eighth inning on his final turn at bat he

This action sequence shows why Brooks Robinson was named the most valuable player in the Series. Here, he makes a diving catch of Johnny Bench's line drive in foul territory in the ninth inning of the final game in Baltimore. He made several "impossible" plays like this one all through the Series.

struck out. The crowd gave him a standing ovation as he went to the dugout. "That was the first time I was ever cheered for striking out," he grinned.

Brooks had hardly left the field when a representative of the National Baseball Hall of Fame was on hand to request his glove for the baseball museum in Cooperstown.

Sparky Anderson won many friends by refusing to alibi even though the Reds' crippled pitching staff gave him a good excuse. "Brooks Robinson beat us," he said. He visited the great third baseman in the clubhouse after the final game and congratulated him.

Of course, Brooks did not do it all by himself. It only seemed that way, he was so outstanding. In the outfield the Orioles pulled down many hard line drives that seemed to be going for sure hits. Sixteen times the Reds smashed screamers into the infield or deep into the outfield, only to see an Oriole make the impossible play — usually Robinson but not always.

"I hope we can meet the Orioles next year," Johnny Bench said. "Maybe Brooks Robinson will retire by then."

Johnny's hope of playing the Birds came to naught in 1971. It was a miserable season for the Reds. They were never in contention and finished a dismal fourth in the league's West Division, 11 games out. What caused the collapse? Injuries, subpar batting and the downfall of Johnny himself. The league's Most Valuable Player in 1970, he batted a puny .238 in 1971, hit only 27 homers (down from 45) and his RBI's sank from 148 to 61.

Things were much brighter in Pittsburg. The Pirates won the National League East Division and conquered the San Francisco Giants in the playoffs. It was a sound club and a happy one under the calm and capable guidance of manager Danny Murtaugh. The Buccaneers came through to a man. Outfielder Roberto Clemente, despite his 37 years, batted a rousing .341. Catcher Manny Sanguillen also stood out with a solid .319 and 81 RBI's, and Willie Stargell, a powerful slugger, led the majors with 48 homers and drove in 125 runs. He played left field or first with the greatest of ease. The Pirate pitching staff was nothing to shout about, however. No hurler won 20 games, but Dock Ellis came close with 19 wins (and nine losses).

In contrast to the Bucs' staff was Baltimore's glittering quartet: Cueller, Palmer and McNally (20-game winners in 1970 and '71) plus newcomer Pat Dobson, who had a 20–8 season, thus giving the Orioles the distinction of having the first quartet of 20-game winners since the White Sox of 1920. The four aces accounted for 81 of the Birds' 101 regular-season victories. The Orioles finished the season with a rush, winning their last 11 games and achieving 100 or more victories for the third year in a row.*

They seemed to have everything and there was talk of a new baseball dynasty, like the Yankees of yore. They had now won three straight pennants and nine consecutive playoff games. (They blanked the Oakland A's in the 1971 playoffs.) They led the league in club batting, fielding and pitching and had the momentum of a 14-game winning streak going for them (11 season games and three playoffs) when they faced the Pirates in the Series opener in Baltimore.

In the first inning Roberto Clemente furnished the only excitement when he drove a double to center off Dave McNally. The hit was meaningless but it caused a slight stir in the press box when the statisticians revealed that the 185-pound Puerto Rican had now hit in eight straight Series games. (He had hit in all seven games back in 1960 when the Pirates defeated the Yankees.)

In the next inning misfortune descended upon the Birds as they presented the Bucs with three unearned runs, thanks to a wild McNally and a leaky Oriole defense, a rare combination. But the Pirates' lead did not last long. Baltimore got one run back in the bottom of the second on Frank Robinson's homer and in the third they clobbered the Bucs with three hits and three runs. They added another run in the fifth making the score, 5–3 and that was it. Now it was 15 straight wins for the Orioles.

They made it 16 straight two days later (Oct. 11) and it was a slaughter. They ran up 11 runs against only three for the Pirates. Brooks Robinson was his old self again. He speared a couple of hot ones and had a perfect day at the plate as he drove in three runs with three singles and walked twice. Oddly, the Birds did not make one extra-base hit. All 14 of their hits were singles.

What could stop them now? The odds against the Pirates making a comeback were out of sight. Roberto was the only one who was hitting consistently. He got two more blows in the second game and stretched his string to nine Series games.

* Only two other teams have won 100 or more games three years in a row: the Philadelphia A's in 1929–'31 and the Cardinals in 1942–'44.

The scene shifted to Three Rivers Stadium in Pittsburgh on October 12 and when Steve Blass walked to the mound as starting pitcher for the Bucs many a head wagged in disapproval. The thin-faced right-hander had not been going so well recently. In the playoffs the Giants had twice shelled him off the mound as he allowed 14 hits in seven innings of toil. His season record was a mediocre 15–8.

But Steve had no trouble handling the World Champions that afternoon. He cooly subdued them and had a no-hitter going until the fifth when Brooks Robinson (who else?) tagged him for a single. But Brooks proved he was human. He was charged with an error in the fifth when a throw got away from him.

The Pirates were ahead, 2–0, in the seventh when Steve made his only mistake by serving a home-run ball to Frank Robinson. It was the Birds' only run. The Bucs got three runs across when they came up in the seventh and made it 5–1, the final score. The Cuban-born Mike Cueller was the loser.

As the triumphant Pirates trotted off the field after the last out an ecstatic fan jumped on the roof of their dugout and began dancing a jig. The cops grabbed him but smilingly let him go when Steve shouted up to them, "Hey, he's my dad." Mr. Blass had come from Connecticut with Steve's mother to see his son win the three-hitter and bring the Pirates half-way back from the grave.

The next day the Bucs came all the way back by squeaking out a 4–3 victory in the first night game in World Series history. A couple of Pirate kids, Bruce Kison and Milt May, were the heroes. Bruce pitched six and one-third innings of one-hit relief ball, and Milt hit a pinch single in the eighth that drove in the winning run. The two 21-year-old rookies were buddies off the field.

The game was played before a full house of 51,378 and was seen by an estimated 63 million viewers, the largest TV audience ever for a prime-time sports event. They saw the gallant Roberto do it again. It was three singles this time.

Manager Danny Murtaugh called upon Nelson (Nellie) Briles to pitch the all-important fifth game, the tie-breaker. Nellie was a question mark. It was his first year with the Bucs and he had but four complete games to his credit. But Nellie was hot that day. He absolutely befuddled the Birds with a two-hitter and blanked them, 4–0. He went all the way and singled in a run in the second. Brooks Robinson, Mr. Golden Glove himself, booted another one and let in a run in the third. It was Balti-

Pirate outfielder Roberto Clemente lashes out his 3,000th hit,* a feat shared only by 10 other players in major-league history. Winner of four N.L. batting crowns, the slugging Puerto Rican hit safely in 14 Series games, in 1960 and 1971. At age 37 he was the star of the '71 Series with his acrobatic catches, two homers, a triple and two doubles for a .414 average.

*Made late in the 1972 season, it was the last hit of his life. He died in a plane crash in Puerto Rico on December 31, 1972. His lifetime batting average of .317 was the highest among all active players. He was voted into the Hall of Fame in 1973 by a special election.

more's ninth Series error. Roberto kept rolling along, with a single in the fifth.

Back to Baltimore went the two clubs, the Pirates riding high on a three-game winning streak, the Birds riding low, one game down and on a scoreless streak of 17 consecutive innings. Maybe that was why there were 9,000 fewer fans in the park than were there for the opener a week earlier. They missed a thriller.

The Bucs got a run in the second and another in the third, but the Birds picked up runs in the fifth and sixth to even the score, 2–2. It stayed that way until the bottom of the 10th, when the Birds came up—and suddenly it was Robinsonville again. Frank Robinson walked and raced to third on a single. Then Brooks Robinson flied to Vic Davalillo in shallow center and Frank took off for home. He just made it by sliding under catcher Sanguillen who had to leap high to snare Davalillo's lofty throw. Thus ended the sixth contest, in a cloud of dust and two men flat on the ground.

Steve Blass and Mike Cueller faced each other for the second time in the October 17 finale before another under-capacity crowd. Both pitchers were sharp and the game turned out to be a sparkling duel—tense and tight throughout.

Mike retired 11 straight batters before the incomparable Roberto homered in the fourth with the bases empty. There was no more scoring until the eighth, when Willie Stargell doubled and drove in a run. The Birds threatened in their half of the eighth with two hits but got only one run across. That made it 2–1 for the Pirates and they kept it that way to become, at last, the World Champions.

Roberto took all the honors. He not only played magnificently in the field, he hit in every game, made 12 in all, including two doubles, a triple and two homers. After the game as he was being praised before the TV cameras, he asked to say a few words to his parents. In genuine humility he said in Spanish: "On this the proudest moment of my life, I ask your blessings."

Not so humble was manager Earl Weaver who insisted that his Orioles were "still the best team in baseball, and we'll prove that next season by winning 100 games for the fourth straight year."

Not quite, Mr. Weaver, not quite. Your Birds did not fly that high in 1972. They won only 80 and sank to third in their division, five games behind first-place Detroit.

The Tigers, however, went down before the Oakland A's in the playoffs, and the Pirates lost out to the Reds for the National League pennant. (Incidentally, this was the first time a team with the second-best winning percentage won the pennant. Cincinnati had a 95–59 record; the Pirates were 96–59, a half-game better.) Both pennant play-offs went the full five-game limit, thus extending the season and delay-ing the start of the Series. Both clubs were bone-weary, injured and reeling when they finally came together in Cincinnati on October 14, the latest date ever for an opener.

The A's were respected around the circuit, despite their flam-boyant, gold-and-emerald uniforms, their handlebar mustaches, leonine manes and their equally flamboyant owner, Charles O. Finley. A self-made multimillionaire, he also owned a pro hockey club and a pro basketball team. He ran all three like a czar, making numerous trades, setting salaries and hiring and firing employees with abandon. On his many travels he sometimes brought along his pet mule mascot in his plane. "The mule," said one baseball official, "is the only thing in his organization with a chance for a pension."

Finley's ball club was young and eager. It had good pitching, passable hitting and fielding—and pitcher Vida Blue, the wonder-boy of 1971, but not of 1972. Vida turned in a dazzling 24–8 performance his rookie year. The next spring he demanded a big raise (from $13,500 to $90,000) but settled for less long after baseball's first players' strike had already delayed the scheduled opening 10 days. When Vida finally joined the A's he was rusty. He sulked, lost his touch and wound up with a dismal 6–10 season.

Back on top again, the Reds were an aggressive, base-running, scrappy club in the National League tradition. Johnny Bench had come back strong after his fall from grace in 1971. He won the league's Most Valuable Player award again, with his 40 homers, .270 batting average and 125 RBI's. Outfielder Pete Rose (.304), often called baseball's most consistent player, topped .300 for the eighth straight season. He was the leadoff man and behind him came the speedsters Joe Morgan and Bobby Tolan, followed by Johnny and his big bat.

Baseball buffs looked for an interesting Series and it turned out to be just that. Many records were shattered, every game was close except one and many things happened that never happened before in any Series. Here are some items:

Six of the seven games were decided by one run (a record); no pitcher completed a game (another record); both clubs batted .209, an

Gene Tenace, Oakland's catcher, slams out a two-run homer in the first game of the 1972 Series, as Johnny Bench squats behind the plate. Johnny was voted MVP of the 1972 season, but Gene took all the honors in the Series, hitting four homers in all, driving in nine runs and averaging .348.

all-time low for seven games; the A's manager, Dick Williams, visited the mound 55 times, a feat that inspired some wag to dub the Series "The Dick Williams Show." And to top it off, the A's catcher, Gene Tenace, who batted only .225 in the season broke Babe Ruth's slugging average with a .913 mark, blasted four homers, drove in nine runs, batted .348 and astounded everybody, including Finley's mule. He wound up playing first and was yanked for a pinch-runner in the final game. Gene won the Series' MVP award and the sports car that went with it.

It was a base-stealing festival for the Reds, who swiped 12 in 15 trys; there were belly-whopper slides, collisions at the plate, some terrible fielding and a brilliant show by the Reds' third sacker, Denis Menke, who accepted 30 chances without an error and proved that Brooks Robinson wasn't the only third baseman in the world.

The A's were the underdogs but they had the edge in pitching and their basic plan was to get out the Reds' first three hitters, so that Johnny Bench, batting behind them, would have nobody to drive home. The plan worked to near-perfection in the first two games, which the A's won, 3–2 and 2–1 on artificial turf in Cincinnati. They were understandably jubilant, knowing that no club had ever come back after losing the first two games on its home grounds.

As all fans and players know, baseball is at its worse when played in twilight. Nevertheless, baseball officialdom allowed the next three Series games to start at twilight for the sake of TV prime time. The Reds fared better in Oakland than at home. They took the third game, 1–0, lost the next one, 3–2 and finished the set with a 5–4 win. Late that night the exhausted players flew to Cincinnati for the sixth game, which was scheduled for the next day. Customarily there is a day off for travel, as there was when the clubs went West to Oakland. But not this time. Again, television called the shots. In any event, the Reds were able to pummel Vida Blue in an 8–1 victory.

The final game was a cliff-hanger that could have gone either way. A frightful three-base error by Bobby Tolan in center and Gene Tenace's bat made the difference. Bobby gave the A's a run and Gene batted in two. It was 3–2, the A's leading in the ninth, with two out when Cincinnati fans were given one final ray of hope. Darrel Chaney with a Series batting average of zero (0 for 7) stood at the plate and got hit on the ankle by Rollie Fingers, the A's top relief pitcher. Pete Rose, a great clutch player, came up as 56,040 fans, the largest crowd ever to see a ball game in Cincinnati, got up roaring, begging him to wallop one. And he almost did. He hit a long drive to left center that looked at first like a homer, but Joe Rudi chased it down and ended the game.

One of the most sensational catches ever made in Series play was Joe Rudi's grab of Denis Menke's ninth-inning drive. The Oakland left fielder made the game-saving catch with a runner on base in the A's 2-1 victory over the Reds on October 15, 1972. A week later he made the last putout of the Series.

WORLD SERIES RECORDS

CLUB BATTING, ONE SERIES
Highest Average: .338, New York A.L., 1960, 7 games (vs. Pittsburgh N.L.)
Lowest Average: .142, Los Angeles N.L., 1966, 4 games (vs. Baltimore A.L.)

MOST RUNS, ONE CLUB, ONE SERIES
55 — New York A.L., 1960, 7 games (vs. Pittsburgh N.L.)

FEWEST RUNS, ONE CLUB, ONE SERIES
3 — Philadelphia A.L., 1905, 5 games (vs. New York N.L.)

MOST HITS, ONE CLUB, ONE GAME
20 — New York N.L., Oct. 7, 1921 (vs. New York A.L.)
    St. Louis N.L., Oct. 10, 1946 (vs. Boston A.L.)

FEWEST HITS, ONE CLUB, ONE GAME
0 — Brooklyn N.L., Oct. 8, 1956, perfect game (vs. New York A.L.)

MOST HOMERS, ONE CLUB, ONE GAME
5 — New York A.L., Oct. 9, 1928 (vs. St. Louis N.L.)

MOST HOMERS, INDIVIDUAL, ONE GAME
3 — Babe Ruth, New York A.L., Oct. 6, 1926, and Oct. 9, 1928 (vs. St. Louis N.L., both games)

MOST HOMERS, INDIVIDUAL, TOTAL SERIES
15 — Babe Ruth, 10 Series, 41 games

MOST SERIES, INDIVIDUAL BATTING .300 OR OVER
6 — Babe Ruth, New York A.L., 1921, 1923, 1926, 1927, 1928, 1932

INDIVIDUAL BATTING, ONE SERIES
Highest Average: .625, Babe Ruth, New York A.L., 1928, 4 games (vs. St. Louis N.L.)

MOST RUNS BATTED IN, INDIVIDUAL, ONE SERIES
12 — Robert C. Richardson, New York A.L., 1960, 7 games (vs. Pittsburgh N.L.)

INDIVIDUAL BATTING, TOTAL SERIES
Highest Average: .363, Frank (Home Run) Baker, Phila. A.L. and New York A.L., 1910–1922,
6 Series, 25 games, 91 at-bats, 33 hits

MOST RUNS, ONE CLUB, ONE GAME

18 — New York A.L., Oct. 2, 1936 (vs. New York N.L.)

MOST RUNS, ONE CLUB, ONE INNING

10 — Philadelphia A.L., Oct. 12, 1929, seventh inning (vs. Chicago N.L.)

MOST STRIKEOUTS BY PITCHER, ONE GAME

14 — Carl D. Erskine, Brooklyn N.L., Oct. 2, 1953 (vs. New York A.L.)

MOST GAMES WON BY PITCHER, LOSING NONE, TOTAL SERIES

6 — Vernon (Lefty) Gomez, New York A.L., 1932, 1936, 1937, 1938

EARLIEST DATE FOR WORLD SERIES GAME

Sept. 5, 1918, Boston A.L. vs. Chicago N.L. at Chicago

LATEST DATE FOR WORLD SERIES GAME

Oct. 26, 1911, Philadelphia A.L. vs. New York N.L. at Philadelphia

LARGEST ATTENDANCE, ONE GAME

92,706 — Oct. 6, 1959, Chicago A.L. vs. Los Angeles N.L., fifth game, at Los Angeles

LARGEST ATTENDANCE, SERIES

420,784 — 1959, Los Angeles N.L. vs. Chicago A.L., 6 games

SMALLEST ATTENDANCE, SERIES

62,232 — 1908, Chicago N.L. vs. Detroit A.L., 5 games

LONGEST GAME BY INNINGS

14 innings — Oct. 9, 1916 (Boston A.L., 2; Brooklyn N.L., 1) at Boston

LONGEST GAME BY TIME, EXTRA INNINGS

3 hours, 28 minutes — Oct. 8, 1945 (Chicago N.L., 8; Detroit A.L., 7) at Chicago, 12 innings

LONGEST NINE-INNING GAME

3 hours, 26 minutes — Oct. 5, 1956 (Brooklyn N.L., 13; New York A.L., 8) at Brooklyn

YOUNGEST AND OLDEST WORLD SERIES PLAYERS

Youngest: Freddie Lindstrom, New York N.L., 18 years, 10 months, 13 days, Oct. 4, 1924, first game (Washington A.L. vs. New York N.L.) at Washington

Oldest: John P. Quinn, Philadelphia A.L., 44 years, 3 months, Oct. 4, 1930, third game (Philadelphia A.L. vs. St. Louis N.L.) at St. Louis

Record of the World Series Games

(1903-1972)

Pitchers named in parenthesis are winners and losers.

1903

	W.	L.
BOSTON A.L.	5	3
PITTSBURGH N.L.	3	5

Oct. 1	Pittsburgh (Phillippe)	7	Boston (Young)	3 At Boston
Oct. 2	Boston (Dinneen)	3	Pittsburgh (Leever)	0 At Boston
Oct. 3	Pittsburgh (Phillippe)	4	Boston (Hughes)	2 At Boston
Oct. 6	Pittsburgh (Phillippe)	5	Boston (Dinneen)	4 At Pittsburgh
Oct. 7	Boston (Young)	11	Pittsburgh (Kennedy)	2 At Pittsburgh
Oct. 8	Boston (Dinneen)	6	Pittsburgh (Leever)	3 At Pittsburgh
Oct. 10	Boston (Young)	7	Pittsburgh (Phillippe)	3 At Pittsburgh
Oct. 13	Boston (Dinneen)	3	Pittsburgh (Phillippe)	0 At Boston

1904

NO SERIES

1905

	W.	L.
NEW YORK N.L.	4	1
PHILADELPHIA A.L.	1	4

Oct. 9	New York (Mathewson)	3	Philadelphia (Plank)	0 At Philadelphia
Oct. 10	Philadelphia (Bender)	3	New York (McGinnity)	0 At New York
Oct. 12	New York (Mathewson)	9	Philadelphia (Coakley)	0 At Philadelphia
Oct. 13	New York (McGinnity)	1	Philadelphia (Plank)	0 At New York
Oct. 14	New York (Mathewson)	2	Philadelphia (Bender)	0 At New York

1906

	W.	L.
CHICAGO A.L.	4	2
CHICAGO N.L.	2	4

Oct. 9	Chicago A (Altrock)	2	Chicago N (Brown)	1 At W. Side Park
Oct. 10	Chicago N (Reulbach)	7	Chicago A (White)	1 At Comiskey Park
Oct. 11	Chicago A (Walsh)	3	Chicago N (Pfiester)	0 At W. Side Park
Oct. 12	Chicago N (Brown)	1	Chicago A (Altrock)	0 At Comiskey Park
Oct. 13	Chicago A (Walsh)	8	Chicago N (Pfiester)	6 At W. Side Park
Oct. 14	Chicago A (White)	8	Chicago N (Brown)	3 At Comiskey Park

1907

	W.	L.	T.
CHICAGO N.L.	4	0	1
DETROIT A.L.	0	4	1

Oct. 8	Chicago (tie)	3	Detroit (tie)	3 At Chicago
Oct. 9	Chicago (Pfiester)	3	Detroit (Mullin)	1 At Chicago
Oct. 10	Chicago (Reulbach)	5	Detroit (Siever)	1 At Chicago
Oct. 11	Chicago (Overall)	6	Detroit (Donovan)	1 At Detroit
Oct. 12	Chicago (Brown)	2	Detroit (Mullin)	0 At Detroit

1908

	W.	L.
CHICAGO N.L.	4	1
DETROIT A.L.	1	4

Oct. 10	Chicago (Brown)	10	Detroit (Summers)	6 At Detroit
Oct. 11	Chicago (Overall)	6	Detroit (Donovan)	1 At Chicago
Oct. 12	Detroit (Mullin)	8	Chicago (Pfiester)	3 At Chicago
Oct. 13	Chicago (Brown)	3	Detroit (Summers)	0 At Detroit
Oct. 14	Chicago (Overall)	2	Detroit (Donovan)	0 At Detroit

1909

	W.	L.
PITTSBURGH N.L.	4	3
DETROIT A.L.	3	4

Oct. 8	Pittsburgh (Adams)	4	Detroit (Mullin)	1 At Pittsburgh
Oct. 9	Detroit (Donovan)	7	Pittsburgh (Camnitz)	2 At Pittsburgh
Oct. 11	Pittsburgh (Maddox)	8	Detroit (Summers)	6 At Detroit
Oct. 12	Detroit (Mullin)	5	Pittsburgh (Leifield)	0 At Detroit
Oct. 13	Pittsburgh (Adams)	8	Detroit (Summers)	4 At Pittsburgh
Oct. 14	Detroit (Mullin)	5	Pittsburgh (Willis)	4 At Detroit
Oct. 16	Pittsburgh (Adams)	8	Detroit (Donovan)	0 At Detroit

1910

	W.	L.
PHILADELPHIA A.L.	4	1
CHICAGO N.L.	1	4

Oct. 17	Philadelphia (Bender)	4	Chicago (Overall)	1 At Philadelphia
Oct. 18	Philadelphia (Coombs)	9	Chicago (Brown)	3 At Philadelphia
Oct. 20	Philadelphia (Coombs)	12	Chicago (McIntire)	5 At Chicago
Oct. 22	Chicago (Brown)	4	Philadelphia (Bender)	3 At Chicago
Oct. 23	Philadelphia (Coombs)	7	Chicago (Brown)	2 At Chicago

1911

	W.	L.
PHILADELPHIA A.L.	4	2
NEW YORK N.L.	2	4

Oct. 14	New York (Mathewson)	2	Philadelphia (Bender)	1 At New York
Oct. 16	Philadelphia (Plank)	3	New York (Marquard)	1 At Philadelphia
Oct. 17	Philadelphia (Coombs)	3	New York (Mathewson)	2 At New York
Oct. 24	Philadelphia (Bender)	4	New York (Mathewson)	2 At Philadelphia
Oct. 25	New York (Crandall)	4	Philadelphia (Plank)	3 At New York
Oct. 26	Philadelphia (Bender)	13	New York (Ames)	2 At Philadelphia

1912

	W.	L.	T.
BOSTON A.L.	4	3	1
NEW YORK N.L.	3	4	1

Oct. 8	Boston (Wood)	4	New York (Tesreau)	3 At New York
Oct. 9	Boston (tie)	6	New York (tie)	6 At Boston
Oct. 10	New York (Marquard)	2	Boston (O'Brien)	1 At Boston
Oct. 11	Boost (Wood)	3	New York (Tesreau)	1 At New York
Oct. 12	Boston (Bedient)	2	New York (Mathewson)	1 At Boston
Oct. 14	New York (Marquard)	5	Boston (O'Brien)	2 At New York
Oct. 15	New York (Tesreau)	11	Boston (Wood)	4 At Boston
Oct. 16	Boston (Wood)	3	New York (Mathewson)	2 At Boston

1913

	W.	L.
PHILADELPHIA A.L.	4	1
NEW YORK N.L.	1	4

Oct. 7	Philadelphia (Bender)	6	New York (Marquard)	4 At New York
Oct. 8	New York (Mathewson)	3	Philadelphia (Plank)	0 At Philadelphia
Oct. 9	Philadelphia (Bush)	8	New York (Tesreau)	2 At New York
Oct. 10	Philadelphia (Bender)	6	New York (Demaree)	5 At Philadelphia
Oct. 11	Philadelphia (Plank)	3	New York (Mathewson)	1 At New York

1914

	W.	L.
BOSTON N.L.	4	0
PHILADELPHIA A.L.	0	4

Oct. 9	Boston (Rudolph)	7	Philadelphia (Bender)	1 At Philadelphia
Oct. 10	Boston (James)	1	Philadelphia (Plank)	0 At Philadelphia
Oct. 12	Boston (James)	5	Philadelphia (Bush)	4 At Boston
Oct. 13	Boston (Rudolph)	3	Philadelphia (Shawkey)	1 At Boston

1915

	W.	L.
BOSTON A.L.	4	1
PHILADELPHIA N.L.	1	4

Oct. 8	Philadelphia (Alexander)	3	Boston (Shore)	1 At Philadelphia
Oct. 9	Boston (Foster)	2	Philadelphia (Mayer)	1 At Philadelphia
Oct. 11	Boston (Leonard)	2	Philadelphia (Alexander)	1 At Boston
Oct. 12	Boston (Shore)	2	Philadelphia (Chalmers)	1 At Boston
Oct. 13	Boston (Foster)	5	Philadelphia (Rixey)	4 At Philadelphia

1916

	W.	L.
BOSTON A.L.	4	1
BROOKLYN N.L.	1	4

Oct. 7	Boston (Shore)	6	Brooklyn (Marquard)	5 At Boston
Oct. 9	Boston (Ruth)	2	Brooklyn (Smith)	1 At Boston
Oct. 10	Brooklyn (Coombs)	4	Boston (Mays)	3 At Brooklyn
Oct. 11	Boston (Leonard)	6	Brooklyn (Marquard)	2 At Brooklyn
Oct. 12	Boston (Shore)	4	Brooklyn (Pfeffer)	1 At Boston

1917

	W.	L.
CHICAGO A.L.	4	2
NEW YORK N.L.	2	4

Oct. 6	Chicago (Cicotte)	2	New York (Sallee)	1 At Chicago
Oct. 7	Chicago (Faber)	7	New York (Anderson)	2 At Chicago
Oct. 10	New York (Benton)	2	Chicago (Cicotte)	0 At New York
Oct. 11	New York (Schupp)	5	Chicago (Faber)	0 At New York
Oct. 13	Chicago (Faber)	8	New York (Sallee)	5 At Chicago
Oct. 15	Chicago (Faber)	4	New York (Benton)	2 At New York

1918

	W.	L.
BOSTON A.L.	4	2
CHICAGO N.L.	2	4

| Sept. 5 | Boston (Ruth) | 1 | Chicago (Vaughn) | 0 At Chicago |
| Sept. 6 | Chicago (Tyler) | 3 | Boston (Bush) | 1 At Chicago |

Sept. 7	Boston (Mays)	2	Chicago (Vaughn)	1 At Chicago
Sept. 9	Boston (Ruth)	3	Chicago (Douglas)	2 At Boston
Sept. 10	Chicago (Vaughn)	3	Boston (Jones)	0 At Boston
Sept. 11	Boston (Mays)	2	Chicago (Tyler)	1 At Boston

1919

	W.	L.
CINCINNATI N.L.	5	3
CHICAGO A.L.	3	5

Oct. 1	Cincinnati (Ruether)	9	Chicago (Cicotte)	1 At Cincinnati
Oct. 2	Cincinnati (Sallee)	4	Chicago (Williams)	2 At Cincinnati
Oct. 3	Chicago (Kerr)	3	Cincinnati (Fisher)	0 At Chicago
Oct. 4	Cincinnati (Ring)	2	Chicago (Cicotte)	0 At Chicago
Oct. 6	Cincinnati (Eller)	5	Chicago (Williams)	0 At Chicago
Oct. 7	Chicago (Kerr)	5	Cincinnati (Ring)	4 At Cincinnati
Oct. 8	Chicago (Cicotte)	4	Cincinnati (Sallee)	1 At Cincinnati
Oct. 9	Cincinnati (Eller)	10	Chicago (Williams)	5 At Chicago

1920

	W.	L.
CLEVELAND A.L.	5	2
BROOKLYN N.L.	2	5

Oct. 5	Cleveland (Coveleskie)	3	Brooklyn (Marquard)	1 At Brooklyn
Oct. 6	Brooklyn (Grimes)	3	Cleveland (Bagby)	0 At Brooklyn
Oct. 7	Brooklyn (Smith)	2	Cleveland (Caldwell)	1 At Brooklyn
Oct. 9	Cleveland (Coveleskie)	5	Brooklyn (Cadore)	1 At Cleveland
Oct. 10	Cleveland (Bagby)	8	Brooklyn (Grimes)	1 At Cleveland
Oct. 11	Cleveland (Mails)	1	Brooklyn (Smith)	0 At Cleveland
Oct. 12	Cleveland (Coveleskie)	3	Brooklyn (Grimes)	0 At Cleveland

1921

	W.	L.
NEW YORK N.L.	5	3
NEW YORK A.L.	3	5

Oct. 5	New York A (Mays)	3	New York N (Nehf)	0 At Polo Grounds
Oct. 6	New York A (Hoyt)	3	New York N (Douglas)	0 At Polo Grounds
Oct. 7	New York N (Barnes)	13	New York A (Quinn)	5 At Polo Grounds
Oct. 9	New York N (Douglas)	4	New York A (Mays)	2 At Polo Grounds
Oct. 10	New York A (Hoyt)	3	New York N (Nehf)	1 At Polo Grounds
Oct. 11	New York N (Barnes)	8	New York A (Shawkey)	5 At Polo Grounds
Oct. 12	New York N (Douglas)	2	New York A (Mays)	1 At Polo Grounds
Oct. 13	New York N (Nehf)	1	New York A (Hoyt)	0 At Polo Grounds

1922

	W.	L.	T.
NEW YORK N.L.	4	0	1
NEW YORK A.L.	0	4	1

Oct. 4	New York N (Ryan)	3	New York A (Bush)	2 At Polo Grounds
Oct. 5	New York N (tie)	3	New York A (tie)	3 At Polo Grounds
Oct. 6	New York N (Scott)	3	New York A (Hoyt)	0 At Polo Grounds
Oct. 7	New York N (McQuillan)	4	New York A (Mays	3 At Polo Grounds
Oct. 8	New York N (Nehf)	5	New York A (Bush)	3 At Polo Grounds

1923

	W.	L.
NEW YORK A.L.	4	2
NEW YORK N.L.	2	4

Oct. 10	New York N (Ryan)	5	New York A (Bush)	4 At Yankee Stadium
Oct. 11	New York A (Pennock)	4	New York N (McQuillan)	2 At Polo Grounds
Oct. 12	New York N (Nehf)	1	New York A (Jones)	0 At Yankee Stadium
Oct. 13	New York A (Shawkey)	8	New York N (Scott)	4 At Polo Grounds
Oct. 14	New York A (Bush)	8	New York N (Bentley)	1 At Yankee Stadium
Oct. 15	New York A (Pennock)	6	New York N (Nehf)	4 At Polo Grounds

1924

	W.	L.
WASHINGTON A.L.	4	3
NEW YORK N.L.	3	4

Oct. 4	New York (Nehf)	4	Washington (Johnson)	3 At Washington
Oct. 5	Washington (Zachary)	4	New York (Bentley)	3 At Washington
Oct. 6	New York (McQuillan)	6	Washington (Marberry)	4 At New York
Oct. 7	Washington (Mogridge)	7	New York (Barnes)	4 At New York
Oct. 8	New York (Bentley)	6	Washington (Johnson)	2 At New York
Oct. 9	Washington (Zachary)	2	New York (Nehf)	1 At Washington
Oct. 10	Washington (Johnson)	4	New York (Bentley)	3 At Washington

1925

	W.	L.
PITTSBURGH N.L.	4	3
WASHINGTON A.L.	3	4

Oct. 7	Washington (Johnson)	4	Pittsburgh (Meadows)	1 At Pittsburgh
Oct. 8	Pittsburgh (Aldridge)	3	Washington (Coveleskie)	2 At Pittsburgh
Oct. 10	Washington (Ferguson)	4	Pittsburgh (Kremer)	3 At Washington
Oct. 11	Washington (Johnson)	4	Pittsburgh (Yde)	0 At Washington
Oct. 12	Pittsburgh (Aldridge)	6	Washington (Coveleskie)	3 At Washington
Oct. 13	Pittsburgh (Kremer)	3	Washington (Ferguson)	2 At Pittsburgh
Oct. 15	Pittsburgh (Kremer)	9	Washington (Johnson)	7 At Pittsburgh

1926

	W.	L.
ST. LOUIS N.L.	4	3
NEW YORK A.L.	3	4

Oct. 2	New York (Pennock)	2	St. Louis (Sherdel)	1 At New York
Oct. 3	St. Louis (Alexander)	6	New York (Shocker)	2 At New York
Oct. 5	St. Louis (Haines)	4	New York (Ruether)	0 At St. Louis
Oct. 6	New York (Hoyt)	10	St. Louis (Reinhart)	5 At St. Louis
Oct. 7	New York (Pennock)	3	St. Louis (Sherdel)	2 At St. Louis
Oct. 9	St. Louis (Alexander)	10	New York (Shawkey)	2 At New York
Oct. 10	St. Louis (Haines)	3	New York (Hoyt)	2 At New York

1927

	W.	L.
NEW YORK A.L.	4	0
PITTSBURGH N.L.	0	4

Oct. 5	New York (Hoyt)	5	Pittsburgh (Kremer)	4 At Pittsburgh
Oct. 6	New York (Pipgras)	6	Pittsburgh (Aldridge)	2 At Pittsburgh
Oct. 7	New York (Pennock)	8	Pittsburgh (Meadows)	1 At New York
Oct. 8	New York (Moore)	4	Pittsburgh (Miljus)	3 At New York

1928

	W.	L.
NEW YORK A.L.	4	0
ST. LOUIS N.L.	0	4

Oct. 4	New York (Hoyt)	4	St. Louis (Sherdel)	1 At New York
Oct. 5	New York (Pipgras)	9	St. Louis (Alexander)	3 At New York
Oct. 7	New York (Zachary)	7	St. Louis (Haines)	3 At St. Louis
Oct. 9	New York (Hoyt)	7	St. Louis (Sherdel)	3 At St. Louis

1929

	W.	L.
PHILADELPHIA A.L.	4	1
CHICAGO N.L.	1	4

Oct. 8	Philadelphia (Ehmke)	3	Chicago (Root)	1 At Chicago
Oct. 9	Philadelphia (Earnshaw)	9	Chicago (Malone)	3 At Chicago
Oct. 11	Chicago (Bush)	3	Philadelphia (Earnshaw)	1 At Philadelphia
Oct. 12	Philadelphia (Rommel)	10	Chicago (Blake)	8 At Philadelphia
Oct. 14	Philadelphia (Walberg)	3	Chicago (Malone)	2 At Philadelphia

1930

	W.	L.
PHILADELPHIA A.L.	4	2
ST. LOUIS N.L.	2	4

Oct. 1	Philadelphia (Grove)	5	St. Louis (Grimes)	2 At Philadelphia
Oct. 2	Philadelphia (Earnshaw)	6	St. Louis (Rhem)	1 At Philadelphia
Oct. 4	St. Louis (Hallahan)	5	Philadelphia (Walberg)	0 At St. Louis
Oct. 5	St. Louis (Haines)	3	Philadelphia (Grove)	1 At St. Louis
Oct. 6	Philadelphia (Grove)	2	St. Louis (Grimes)	0 At St. Louis
Oct. 8	Philadelphia (Earnshaw)	8	St. Louis (Hallahan)	1 At Philadelphia

1931

	W.	L.
ST. LOUIS N.L.	4	3
PHILADELPHIA A.L.	3	4

Oct. 1	Philadelphia (Grove)	6	St. Louis (Derringer)	2 At St. Louis
Oct. 2	St. Louis (Hallahan)	2	Philadelphia (Earnshaw)	0 At St. Louis
Oct. 5	St. Louis (Grimes)	5	Philadelphia (Grove)	2 At Philadelphia
Oct. 6	Philadelphia (Earnshaw)	3	St. Louis (Johnson)	0 At Philadelphia
Oct. 7	St. Louis (Hallahan)	5	Philadelphia (Hoyt)	1 At Philadelphia
Oct. 9	Philadelphia (Grove)	8	St. Louis (Derringer)	1 At St. Louis
Oct. 10	St. Louis (Grimes)	4	Philadelphia (Earnshaw)	2 At St. Louis

1932

	W.	L.
NEW YORK A.L.	4	0
CHICAGO N.L.	0	4

Sept. 28	New York (Ruffing)	12	Chicago (Bush)	6 At New York
Sept. 29	New York (Gomez)	5	Chicago (Warneke)	2 At New York
Oct. 1	New York (Pipgras)	7	Chicago (Root)	5 At Chicago
Oct. 2	New York (Moore)	13	Chicago (May)	6 At Chicago

1933

		W.	L.
NEW YORK N.L.		4	1
WASHINGTON A.L.		1	4

Oct. 3	New York (Hubbell)	4	Washington (Stewart)	2	At New York
Oct. 4	New York (Schumacher)	6	Washington (Crowder)	1	At New York
Oct. 5	Washington (Whitehill)	4	New York (Fitzsimmons)	0	At Washington
Oct. 6	New York (Hubbell)	2	Washington (Weaver)	1	At Washington
Oct. 7	New York (Luque)	4	Washington (Russell)	3	At Washington

1934

		W.	L.
ST. LOUIS N.L.		4	3
DETROIT A.L.		3	4

Oct. 3	St. Louis (J. Dean)	8	Detroit (Crowder)	3	At Detroit
Oct. 4	Detroit (Rowe)	3	St. Louis (W. Walker)	2	At Detroit
Oct. 5	St. Louis (P. Dean)	4	Detroit (Bridges)	1	At St. Louis
Oct. 6	Detroit (Auker)	10	St. Louis (W. Walker)	4	At St. Louis
Oct. 7	Detroit (Bridges)	3	St. Louis (J. Dean)	1	At St. Louis
Oct. 8	St. Louis (P. Dean)	4	Detroit (Rowe)	3	At Detroit
Oct. 9	St. Louis (J. Dean)	11	Detroit (Auker)	0	At Detroit

1935

		W.	L.
DETROIT A.L.		4	2
CHICAGO N.L.		2	4

Oct. 2	Chicago (Warneke)	3	Detroit (Rowe)	0	At Detroit
Oct. 3	Detroit (Bridges)	8	Chicago (Root)	3	At Detroit
Oct. 4	Detroit (Rowe)	6	Chicago (French)	5	At Chicago
Oct. 5	Detroit (Crowder)	2	Chicago (Carleton)	1	At Chicago
Oct. 6	Chicago (Warneke)	3	Detroit (Rowe)	1	At Chicago
Oct. 7	Detroit (Bridges)	4	Chicago (French)	3	At Detroit

1936

		W.	L.
NEW YORK A.L.		4	2
NEW YORK N.L.		2	4

Sept. 30	New York N (Hubbell)	6	New York A (Ruffing)	1	At Polo Grounds
Oct. 2	New York A (Gomez)	18	New York N (Schumacher)	4	At Polo Grounds
Oct. 3	New York A (Hadley)	2	New York N (Fitzsimmons)	1	At Yankee Stadium
Oct. 4	New York A (Pearson)	5	New York N (Hubbell)	2	At Yankee Stadium
Oct. 5	New York N (Schumacher)	5	New York (A) Malone	4	At Yankee Stadium
Oct. 6	New York A (Gomez)	13	New York N (Fitzsimmons)	5	At Polo Grounds

1937

		W.	L.
NEW YORK A.L.		4	1
NEW YORK N.L.		1	4

Oct. 6	New York A (Gomez)	8	New York N (Hubbell)	1	At Yankee Stadium
Oct. 7	New York A (Ruffing)	8	New York N (Melton)	1	At Yankee Stadium
Oct. 8	New York A (Pearson)	5	New York N (Schumacher)	1	At Polo Grounds
Oct. 9	New York N (Hubbell)	7	New York A (Hadley)	3	At Polo Grounds
Oct. 10	New York A (Gomez)	4	New York N (Melton)	2	At Polo Grounds

1938

		W.	L.
NEW YORK A.L.		4	0
CHICAGO N.L.		0	4

Oct. 5	New York (Ruffing)	3	Chicago (Lee)	1 At Chicago
Oct. 6	New York (Gomez)	6	Chicago (Dean)	3 At Chicago
Oct. 8	New York (Pearson)	5	Chicago (Bryant)	2 At New York
Oct. 9	New York (Ruffing)	8	Chicago (Lee)	3 At New York

1939

		W.	L.
NEW YORK A.L.		4	0
CINCINNATI N.L.		0	4

Oct. 4	New York (Ruffing)	2	Cincinnati (Derringer)	1 At New York
Oct. 5	New York (Pearson)	4	Cincinnati (Walters)	0 At New York
Oct. 7	New York (Hadley)	7	Cincinnati (Thompson)	3 At Cincinnati
Oct. 8	New York (Murphy)	7	Cincinnati (Walters)	4 At Cincinnati

1940

		W.	L.
CINCINNATI N.L.		4	3
DETROIT A.L.		3	4

Oct. 2	Detroit (Newsom)	7	Cincinnati (Derringer)	2 At Cincinnati
Oct. 3	Cincinnati (Walters)	5	Detroit (Rowe)	3 At Cincinnati
Oct. 4	Detroit (Bridges)	7	Cincinnati (Turner)	4 At Detroit
Oct. 5	Cincinnati (Derringer)	5	Detroit (Trout)	2 At Detroit
Oct. 6	Detroit (Newsom)	8	Cincinnati (Thompson)	0 At Detroit
Oct. 7	Cincinnati (Walters)	4	Detroit (Rowe)	0 At Cincinnati
Oct. 8	Cincinnati (Derringer)	2	Detroit (Newsom)	1 At Cincinnati

1941

		W.	L.
NEW YORK A.L.		4	1
BROOKLYN N.L.		1	4

Oct. 1	New York (Ruffing)	3	Brooklyn (Davis)	2 At New York
Oct. 2	Brooklyn (Wyatt)	3	New York (Chandler)	2 At New York
Oct. 4	New York (Russo)	2	Brooklyn (Casey)	1 At Brooklyn
Oct. 5	New York (Murphy)	7	Brooklyn (Casey)	4 At Brooklyn
Oct. 6	New York (Bonham)	3	Brooklyn (Wyatt)	1 At Brooklyn

1942

		W.	L.
ST. LOUIS N.L.		4	1
NEW YORK A.L.		1	4

Sept. 30	New York (Ruffing)	7	St. Louis (M. Cooper)	4 At St. Louis
Oct. 1	St. Louis (Beazley)	4	New York (Bonham)	3 At St. Louis
Oct. 3	St. Louis (White)	2	New York (Chandler)	0 At New York
Oct. 4	St. Louis (Lanier)	9	New York (Donald)	6 At New York
Oct. 5	St. Louis (Beazley)	4	New York (Ruffing)	2 At New York

1943

	W.	L.
NEW YORK A.L.	4	1
ST. LOUIS N.L.	1	4

Oct. 5	New York (Chandler)	4	St. Louis (Lanier) .... 2 At New York
Oct. 6	St. Louis (M. Cooper)	4	New York (Bonham) .... 3 At New York
Oct. 7	New York (Borowy)	6	St. Louis (Brazle) .... 2 At New York
Oct. 10	New York (Russo)	2	St. Louis (Brecheen) .... 1 At St. Louis
Oct. 11	New York (Chandler)	2	St. Louis (M. Cooper) .... 0 At St. Louis

1944

	W.	L.
ST. LOUIS N.L.	4	2
ST. LOUIS A.L.	2	4

Oct. 4	St. Louis A (Galehouse)	2	St. Louis N (M. Cooper) ... 1 At Sportsman's Pk.
Oct. 5	St. Louis N (Donnelly)	3	St. Louis A (Muncrief) ...... 2 At Sportsman's Pk.
Oct. 6	St. Louis A (Kramer)	6	St. Louis N (Wilks) .... 2 At Sportsman's Pk.
Oct. 7	St. Louis N (Brecheen)	5	St. Louis A (Jakucki) .... 1 At Sportsman's Pk.
Oct. 8	St. Louis N (M. Cooper)	2	St. Louis A (Galehouse) .... 0 At Sportsman's Pk.
Oct. 9	St. Louis N (Lanier)	3	St. Louis A (Potter) .... 1 At Sportsman's Pk.

1945

	W.	L.
DETROIT A.L.	4	3
CHICAGO N.L.	3	4

Oct. 3	Chicago (Borowy)	9	Detroit (Newhouser) .... 0 At Detroit
Oct. 4	Detroit (Trucks)	4	Chicago (Wyse) .... 1 At Detroit
Oct. 5	Chicago (Passeau)	3	Detroit (Overmire) .... 0 At Detroit
Oct. 6	Detroit (Trout)	4	Chicago (Prim) .... 1 At Chicago
Oct. 7	Detroit (Newhouser)	8	Chicago (Borowy) .... 4 At Chicago
Oct. 8	Chicago (Borowy)	8	Detroit (Trout) .... 7 At Chicago
Oct. 10	Detroit (Newhouser)	9	Chicago (Borowy) .... 3 At Chicago

1946

	W.	L.
ST. LOUIS N.L.	4	3
BOSTON A.L.	3	4

Oct. 6	Boston (Johnson)	3	St. Louis (Pollet) .... 2 At St. Louis
Oct. 7	St. Louis (Brecheen)	3	Boston (Harris) .... 0 At St. Louis
Oct. 9	Boston (Ferriss)	4	St. Louis (Dickson) .... 0 At Boston
Oct. 10	St. Louis (Munger)	12	Boston (Hughson) .... 3 At Boston
Oct. 11	Boston (Dobson)	6	St. Louis (Brazle) .... 3 At Boston
Oct. 13	St. Louis (Brecheen)	4	Boston (Harris) .... 1 At St. Louis
Oct. 15	St. Louis (Brecheen)	4	Boston (Klinger) .... 3 At St. Louis

1947

	W.	L.
NEW YORK A.L.	4	3
BROOKLYN N.L.	3	4

Sept. 30	New York (Shea)	5	Brooklyn (Branca) .... 3 At New York
Oct. 1	New York (Reynolds)	10	Brooklyn (Lombardi) .... 3 At New York

Oct.	2	Brooklyn (Casey)	9	New York (Newsom)	8 At Brooklyn
Oct.	3	Brooklyn (Casey)	3	New York (Bevens)	2 At Brooklyn
Oct.	4	New York (Shea)	2	Brooklyn (Barney)	1 At Brooklyn
Oct.	5	Brooklyn (Branca)	8	New York (Page)	6 At New York
Oct.	6	New York (Page)	5	Brooklyn (Gregg)	2 At New York

1948

		W.	L.
CLEVELAND A.L.		4	2
BOSTON N.L.		2	4

Oct.	6	Boston (Sain)	1	Cleveland (Feller)	0 At Boston
Oct.	7	Cleveland (Lemon)	4	Boston (Spahn)	1 At Boston
Oct.	8	Cleveland (Bearden)	2	Boston (Bickford)	0 At Cleveland
Oct.	9	Cleveland (Gromek)	2	Boston (Sain)	1 At Cleveland
Oct.	10	Boston (Spahn)	11	Cleveland (Feller)	5 At Cleveland
Oct.	11	Cleveland (Lemon)	4	Boston (Voiselle)	3 At Boston

1949

		W.	L.
NEW YORK A.L.		4	1
BROOKLYN N.L.		1	4

Oct.	5	New York (Reynolds)	1	Brooklyn (Newcombe)	0 At New York
Oct.	6	Brooklyn (Roe)	1	New York (Raschi)	0 At New York
Oct.	7	New York (Page)	4	Brooklyn (Branca)	3 At Brooklyn
Oct.	8	New York (Lopat)	6	Brooklyn (Newcombe)	4 At Brooklyn
Oct.	9	New York (Raschi)	10	Brooklyn (Barney)	6 At Brooklyn

1950

		W.	L.
NEW YORK A.L.		4	0
PHILADELPHIA N.L.		0	4

Oct.	4	New York (Raschi)	1	Philadelphia (Konstanty)	0 At Philadelphia
Oct.	5	New York (Reynolds)	2	Philadelphia (Roberts)	1 At Philadelphia
Oct.	6	New York (Ferrick)	3	Philadelphia (Meyer)	2 At New York
Oct.	7	New York (Ford)	5	Philadelphia (Miller)	2 At New York

1951

		W.	L.
NEW YORK A.L.		4	2
NEW YORK N.L.		2	4

Oct.	4	New York N (Koslo)	5	New York A (Reynolds)	1 At Yankee Stadium
Oct.	5	New York A (Lopat)	3	New York N (Jansen)	1 At Yankee Stadium
Oct.	6	New York N (Hearn)	6	New York A (Raschi)	2 At Polo Grounds
Oct.	8	New York A (Reynolds)	6	New York N (Maglie)	2 At Polo Grounds
Oct.	9	New York A (Lopat)	13	New York N (Jansen)	1 At Polo Grounds
Oct.	10	New York A (Raschi)	4	New York N (Koslo)	3 At Yankee Stadium

1952

		W.	L.
NEW YORK A.L.		4	3
BROOKLYN N.L.		3	4

| Oct. | 1 | Brooklyn (Black) | 4 | New York (Reynolds) | 2 At Brooklyn |
| Oct. | 2 | New York (Raschi) | 7 | Brooklyn (Erskine) | 1 At Brooklyn |

Oct. 3	Brooklyn (Roe)	5	New York (Lopat)	3 At New York
Oct. 4	New York (Reynolds)	2	Brooklyn (Black)	0 At New York
Oct. 5	Brooklyn (Erskine)	6	New York (Sain)	5 At New York
Oct. 6	New York (Raschi)	3	Brooklyn (Loes)	2 At Brooklyn
Oct. 7	New York (Reynolds)	4	Brooklyn (Black)	2 At Brooklyn

1953

	W.	L.
NEW YORK A.L.	4	2
BROOKLYN N.L.	2	4

Sept. 30	New York (Sain)	9	Brooklyn (Labine)	5 At New York
Oct. 1	New York (Lopat)	4	Brooklyn (Roe)	2 At New York
Oct. 2	Brooklyn (Erskine)	3	New York (Raschi)	2 At Brooklyn
Oct. 3	Brooklyn (Loes)	7	New York (Ford)	3 At Brooklyn
Oct. 4	New York (McDonald)	11	Brooklyn (Podres)	7 At Brooklyn
Oct. 5	New York (Reynolds)	4	Brooklyn (Labine)	3 At New York

1954

	W.	L.
NEW YORK N.L.	4	0
CLEVELAND A.L.	0	4

Sept. 29	New York (Grissom)	5	Cleveland (Lemon)	2 At New York
Sept. 30	New York (Antonelli)	3	Cleveland (Wynn)	1 At New York
Oct. 1	New York (Gomez)	6	Cleveland (Garcia)	2 At Cleveland
Oct. 2	New York (Liddle)	7	Cleveland (Lemon)	4 At Cleveland

1955

	W.	L.
BROOKLYN N.L.	4	3
NEW YORK A.L.	3	4

Sept. 28	New York (Ford)	6	Brooklyn (Newcombe)	5 At New York
Sept. 29	New York (Byrne)	4	Brooklyn (Loes)	2 At New York
Sept. 30	Brooklyn (Podres)	8	New York (Turley)	3 At Brooklyn
Oct. 1	Brooklyn (Labine)	8	New York (Larsen)	5 At Brooklyn
Oct. 2	Brooklyn (Craig)	5	New York (Grim)	3 At Brooklyn
Oct. 3	New York (Ford)	5	Brooklyn (Spooner)	1 At New York
Oct. 4	Brooklyn (Podres)	2	New York (Byrne)	0 At New York

1956

	W.	L.
NEW YORK A.L.	4	3
BROOKLYN N.L.	3	4

Oct. 3	Brooklyn (Maglie)	6	New York (Ford)	3 At Brooklyn
Oct. 5	Brooklyn (Bessent)	13	New York (Morgan)	8 At Brooklyn
Oct. 6	New York (Ford)	5	Brooklyn (Craig)	3 At New York
Oct. 7	New York (Sturdivant)	6	Brooklyn (Erskine)	2 At New York
Oct. 8	New York (Larsen)	2	Brooklyn (Maglie)	0 At New York
Oct. 9	Brooklyn (Labine)	1	New York (Turley)	0 At Brooklyn
Oct. 10	New York (Kucks)	9	Brooklyn (Newcombe)	0 At Brooklyn

1957

	W.	L.
MILWAUKEE N.L.	4	3
NEW YORK A.L.	3	4

Oct.	2	New York (Ford)	3	Milwaukee (Spahn)	1	At New York
Oct.	3	Milwaukee (Burdette)	4	New York (Shantz)	2	At New York
Oct.	5	New York (Larsen)	12	Milwaukee (Buhl)	3	At Milwaukee
Oct.	6	Milwaukee (Spahn)	7	New York (Grim)	5	At Milwaukee
Oct.	7	Milwaukee (Burdette)	1	New York (Ford)	0	At Milwaukee
Oct.	9	New York (Turley)	3	Milwaukee (Johnson)	2	At New York
Oct.	10	Milwaukee (Burdette)	5	New York (Larsen)	0	At New York

1958

	W.	L.
NEW YORK A.L.	4	3
MILWAUKEE N.L.	3	4

Oct.	1	Milwaukee (Spahn)	4	New York (Duren)	3	At Milwaukee
Oct.	2	Milwaukee (Burdette)	13	New York (Turley)	5	At Milwaukee
Oct.	4	New York (Larsen)	4	Milwaukee (Rush)	0	At New York
Oct.	5	Milwaukee (Spahn)	3	New York (Ford)	0	At New York
Oct.	6	New York (Turley)	7	Milwaukee (Burdette)	0	At Milwaukee
Oct.	8	New York (Duren)	4	Milwaukee (Spahn)	3	At Milwaukee
Oct.	9	New York (Turley)	6	Milwaukee (Burdette)	2	At Milwaukee

1959

	W.	L.
LOS ANGELES N.L.	4	2
CHICAGO A.L.	2	4

Oct.	1	Chicago (Wynn)	11	Los Angeles (Craig)	0	At Chicago
Oct.	2	Los Angeles (Podres)	4	Chicago (Shaw)	3	At Chicago
Oct.	4	Los Angeles (Drysdale)	3	Chicago (Donovan)	1	At Los Angeles
Oct.	5	Los Angeles (Sherry)	5	Chicago (Staley)	4	At Los Angeles
Oct.	6	Chicago (Shaw)	1	Los Angeles (Koufax)	0	At Los Angeles
Oct.	8	Los Angeles (Sherry)	9	Chicago (Wynn)	3	At Chicago

1960

	W.	L.
PITTSBURGH N.L.	4	3
NEW YORK A.L.	3	4

Oct.	5	Pittsburgh (Law)	6	New York (Ditmar)	4	At Pittsburgh
Oct.	6	New York (Turley)	16	Pittsburgh (Friend)	3	At Pittsburgh
Oct.	8	New York (Ford)	10	Pittsburgh (Mizell)	0	At New York
Oct.	9	Pittsburgh (Law)	3	New York (Terry)	2	At New York
Oct.	10	Pittsburgh (Haddix)	5	New York (Ditmar)	2	At New York
Oct.	12	New York (Ford)	12	Pittsburgh (Friend)	0	At Pittsburgh
Oct.	13	Pittsburgh (Haddix)	10	New York (Terry)	9	At Pittsburgh

1961

	W.	L.
NEW YORK A.L.	4	1
CINCINNATI N.L.	1	4

Oct. 4	New York (Ford)	2	Cincinnati (O'Toole)	0 At New York
Oct. 5	Cincinnati (Jay)	6	New York (Terry)	2 At New York
Oct. 7	New York (Arroyo)	3	Cincinnati (Purkey)	2 At Cincinnati
Oct. 8	New York (Ford)	7	Cincinnati (O'Toole)	0 At Cincinnati
Oct. 9	New York (Daley)	13	Cincinnati (Jay)	5 At Cincinnati

1962

	W.	L.
NEW YORK A.L.	4	3
SAN FRANCISCO N.L.	3	4

Oct. 4	New York (Ford)	6	San Francisco (O'Dell)	2 At San Francisco
Oct. 5	San Francisco (Sanford)	2	New York (Terry)	0 At San Francisco
Oct. 7	New York (Stafford)	3	San Francisco (Pierce)	2 At New York
Oct. 8	San Francisco (Larsen)	7	New York (Coates)	3 At New York
Oct. 10	New York (Terry)	5	San Francisco (Sanford)	3 At New York
Oct. 15	San Francisco (Pierce)	5	New York (Ford)	2 At San Francisco
Oct. 16	New York (Terry)	1	San Francisco (Sanford)	0 At San Francisco

1963

	W.	L.
LOS ANGELES N.L.	4	0
NEW YORK A.L.	0	4

Oct. 2	Los Angeles (Koufax)	5	New York (Ford)	2 At New York
Oct. 3	Los Angeles (Podres)	4	New York (Downing)	1 At New York
Oct. 5	Los Angeles (Drysdale)	1	New York (Bouton)	0 At Los Angeles
Oct. 6	Los Angeles (Koufax)	2	New York (Ford)	1 At Los Angeles

1964

	W.	L.
ST. LOUIS N.L.	4	3
NEW YORK A.L.	3	4

Oct. 7	St. Louis (Sadecki)	9	New York (Ford)	5 At St. Louis
Oct. 8	New York (Stottlemyre)	8	St. Louis (Gibson)	3 At St. Louis
Oct. 10	New York (Bouton)	2	St. Louis (Schultz)	1 At New York
Oct. 11	St. Louis (Craig)	4	New York (Downing)	3 At New York
Oct. 12	St. Louis (Gibson)	5	New York (Mikkelsen)	2 At New York
Oct. 14	New York (Bouton)	8	St. Louis (Simmons)	3 At St. Louis
Oct. 15	St. Louis (Gibson)	7	New York (Stottlemyre)	5 At St. Louis

1965

	W.	L.
LOS ANGELES N.L.	4	3
MINNESOTA A.L.	3	4

Oct. 6	Minnesota (Grant)	8	Los Angeles (Drysdale)	2	At Minnesota
Oct. 7	Minnesota (Kaat)	5	Los Angeles (Koufax)	1	At Minnesota
Oct. 9	Los Angeles (Osteen)	4	Minnesota (Pascual)	0	At Los Angeles
Oct. 10	Los Angeles (Drysdale)	7	Minnesota (Grant)	2	At Los Angeles
Oct. 11	Los Angeles (Koufax)	7	Minnesota (Kaat)	0	At Los Angeles
Oct. 13	Minnesota (Grant)	5	Los Angeles (Osteen)	1	At Minnesota
Oct. 14	Los Angeles (Koufax)	2	Minnesota (Kaat)	0	At Minnesota

1966

	W.	L.
BALTIMORE A.L.	4	0
LOS ANGELES N.L.	0	4

Oct. 5	Baltimore (Drabowski)	5	Los Angeles (Drysdale)	2	At Los Angeles
Oct. 6	Baltimore (Palmer)	6	Los Angeles (Koufax)	0	At Los Angeles
Oct. 8	Baltimore (Bunker)	1	Los Angeles (Osteen)	0	At Baltimore
Oct. 9	Baltimore (McNally)	1	Los Angeles (Drysdale)	0	At Baltimore

1967

	W.	L.
ST. LOUIS N.L.	4	3
BOSTON A.L.	3	4

Oct. 4	St. Louis (Gibson)	2	Boston (Santiago)	1	At Boston
Oct. 5	Boston (Lonborg)	5	St. Louis (Hughes)	0	At Boston
Oct. 7	St. Louis (Briles)	5	Boston (Bell)	2	At St. Louis
Oct. 8	St. Louis (Gibson)	6	Boston (Santiago)	0	At St. Louis
Oct. 9	Boston (Lonborg)	3	St. Louis (Carlton)	1	At St. Louis
Oct. 11	Boston (Wyatt)	8	St. Louis (Lamabe)	4	At Boston
Oct. 12	St. Louis (Gibson)	7	Boston (Lonborg)	2	At Boston

1968

	W.	L.
DETROIT A.L.	4	3
ST. LOUIS N.L.	3	4

Oct. 2	St. Louis (Gibson)	4	Detroit (McLain)	0	At St. Louis
Oct. 3	Detroit (Lolich)	8	St. Louis (Briles)	1	At St. Louis
Oct. 5	St. Louis (Washburn)	7	Detroit (Wilson)	3	At Detroit
Oct. 6	St. Louis (Gibson)	10	Detroit (McLain)	1	At Detroit
Oct. 7	Detroit (Lolich)	5	St. Louis (Hoerner)	3	At Detroit
Oct. 9	Detroit (McLain)	13	St. Louis (Washburn)	1	At St. Louis
Oct. 10	Detroit (Lolich)	4	St. Louis (Gibson)	1	At St. Louis

1969

	W.	L.
NEW YORK N.L.	4	1
BALTIMORE A.L.	1	4

Oct. 11	Baltimore (Cuellar)	4	New York (Seaver)	1	At Baltimore
Oct. 12	New York (Koosman)	2	Baltimore (McNally)	1	At Baltimore
Oct. 14	New York (Gentry)	5	Baltimore (Palmer)	0	At New York
Oct. 15	New York (Seaver)	2	Baltimore (Hall)	1	At New York
Oct. 16	New York (Koosman)	5	Baltimore (Watt)	3	At New York

1970

	W.	L.
BALTIMORE A.L.	4	1
CINCINNATI N.L.	1	4

Oct. 10	Baltimore (Palmer)	4	Cincinnati (Nolan)	3	At Cincinnati
Oct. 11	Baltimore (Phoebus)	6	Cincinnati (Wilcox)	5	At Cincinnati
Oct. 13	Baltimore (McNally)	9	Cincinnati (Cloninger)	3	At Baltimore
Oct. 14	Cincinnati (Carroll)	6	Baltimore (Watt)	5	At Baltimore
Oct. 15	Baltimore (Cuellar)	9	Cincinnati (Merritt)	3	At Baltimore

1971

	W.	L.
PITTSBURG N.L.	4	3
BALTIMORE A.L.	3	4

Oct. 9	Baltimore (McNally)	5	Pittsburg (Ellis)	3	At Baltimore
Oct. 11	Baltimore (Palmer)	11	Pittsburg (R. Johnson)	3	At Baltimore
Oct. 12	Pittsburg (Blass)	5	Baltimore (Cuellar)	1	At Pittsburg
Oct. 13	Pittsburg (Kison)	4	Baltimore (Watt)	3	At Pittsburg
Oct. 14	Pittsburg (Briles)	4	Baltimore (McNally)	0	At Pittsburg
Oct. 16	Baltimore (McNally)	3	Pittsburg (Miller)	2	At Baltimore
Oct. 17	Pittsburg (Blass)	2	Baltimore (Cueller)	1	At Baltimore

1972

	W.	L.
OAKLAND A.L.	4	3
CINCINNATI N.L.	3	4

Oct. 14	Oakland (Holtzman)	3	Cincinnati (Nolan)	2	At Cincinnati
Oct. 15	Oakland (Hunter)	2	Cincinnati (Grimsley)	1	At Cincinnati
Oct. 18	Cincinnati (Billingham)	1	Oakland (Odom)	0	At Oakland
Oct. 19	Oakland (Fingers)	3	Cincinnati (Carrol)	2	At Oakland
Oct. 20	Cincinnati (Grimsley)	5	Oakland (Fingers)	4	At Oakland
Oct. 21	Cincinnati (Grimsley)	8	Oakland (Blue)	1	At Cincinnati
Oct. 22	Oakland (Hunter)	3	Cincinnati (Borbon)	2	At Cincinnati

INDEX

217

Cy Young Memorial Award, 137, 179

219

223

Swoboda, Ron, 185

Tenace, Gene, 196, 197
Terry, Bill, 81-82
Terry, Ralph, 154, 161, 162
Thomson, Bobby, 125, 126, 127, 154, 160
Tiger Stadium, 180
Tigers, Detroit, *see* Detroit Tigers
Tinker, Joe, 21, 26
Tolan, Bobby, 195, 197
Toney, Fred, 60
"Tooth" sign, Stallings', 36
Topping, Dan, 109, 120, 127, 155
Torre, Frank, 146
Tresh, Tom, 161, 167
Twins, Minnesota, *see* Minnesota Twins
Turley, Bob, 143, 148, 153
Tyler, Lefty, 36, 37, 38, 39

Veeck, Bill, 147
Virdon, Bill, 153

Waddell, Rube, 16, 17, 20
Wagner, Hans, 27, 28, 29, 30
Walberg, Rube, 75, 79
Walker, Dixie, 114
Walker, Harry (The Hat), 111
Walters, Bucky, 101
Wambsganss, Bill, 59
Washington Senators, 64; vs. New York Giants, 64-66 (*1924*), 82 (*1933*); vs. Pittsburgh Pirates, 67 (*1925*)
Weaver, Buck, 49, 50, 54
Weaver, Earl, 194
Webb, Del, 109
Weiss, George, 169
Wertz, Vic, 132
White, Ernie, 105
White Sox, Chicago, *see* Chicago White Sox
White Stockings, Chicago, 9
Whiteman, George, 47-48
"Whiz Kids," 122-124
Williams, Claude, 49, 50, 51, 53
Williams, Dick, 197
Williams, Ted, 110, 111, 137
Willis, Vic, 30
Wills, Maury, 159, 160 *n.*
Wilson, Hack, 75, 76
Wilson, Jimmy, 101, 102
Witt, Whitey, 61

World Series, 7-8, 158; beginning of, 9-10; (*1905*), 11-21; (*1906*), 23-24; (*1907*), 24-26; (*1908*), 26-27; (*1909*), 27-30; (*1910*), 30-31; (*1911*), 31-32; (*1912*), 32-33; (*1913*), 33; (*1914*), 38-40; (*1915*), 42; (*1916*), 43-44; (*1917*), 45-46; (*1918*), 46-48; (*1919*), 48-53; (*1920*), 57, 58-59; (*1921*), 59-60; (*1922*), 60-61; (*1923*), 63; (*1924*), 64-66; (*1925*), 67; (*1926*), 68-71; (*1927*), 72; (*1928*), 72; (*1929*), 75-77; (*1930*), 78; (*1931*), 79-80; (*1932*), 81; (*1933*), 82; (*1934*), 84-85; (*1935*), 85; (*1936*), 90-92; (*1937*), 92; (*1938*), 95; (*1939*), 98-99; (*1940*), 101-102; (*1941*), 102-104; (*1942*), 105; (*1943*), 105; (*1944*), 106; (*1945*), 106-109; (*1946*), 110-111; (*1947*), 114-117; (*1948*), 117-120; (*1949*), 121-122; (1950), 124; (1951), 126-127; (*1952*), 128-129; (*1953*), 129-130; (*1954*), 132-133; (*1955*), 134-137; (*1956*), 137-140; (*1957*), 142-145; (*1958*), 145-146; (*1959*), 148-150; (*1960*), 151-155; (*1961*), 157-158; (*1962*), 160-163; (*1963*), 164-169; (*1964*), 169-171; (*1965*), 172-173; (*1966*), 173-174; (*1967*), 175-178; (*1968*), 178-181; (*1969*), 183-186; (*1970*), 186-190; (*1971*) 191-194; (*1972*) 195-198; and first-division teams' share of money, 48; players' share of gate receipts in, 24-26; split of players' purse in, 17 and *n.*, 18
Wrigley, William, 81
Wrigley Field, 75, 108
Wynn, Early, 132, 148

Yankee Stadium, 60, 61, 63, 68, 89, 105, 134, 140, 142, 143, 144, 145, 156, 166, 170
Yankees, New York, *see* New York Yankees
Yastrzemski, Carl (Yaz), 175, 176, 178
York, Rudy, 101, 107, 110
Young, Cy, 64
Youngs, Ross, 60, 61

Zimmerman, Heinie, 45, 46

224